ARCADE
GAME
TYPOGRAPHY

ARCADE
GAME
TYPOGRAPHY
THE ART OF PIXEL TYPE

TOSHI OMAGARI

FOREWORD
KIYONORI MUROGA

T&H

TYPEFACES

ESSAYS

KIYONORI
MUROGA
FOREWORD

Typefaces are ubiquitous in our contemporary information environment. Today's highly developed computers and display devices let you use the very same typefaces on screen as for printing. But under the contemporary information surface you can still find legacies of the bitmap typefaces that were unique to 8- or 16-bit computers before the dominance of Microsoft and Apple. Designed to work at low resolution and with limited machine power, such bitmap typefaces may look identical, but they were functional for their own specific purposes – achieving a kind of technological beauty that is still apparent today.

Beyond technological typefaces, there were other genres of bitmap typefaces that were full of diversity, particularly in the world of videogames. Driven by play and imagination, videogame typefaces evolved in a unique profusion during the golden age of arcade games, which lasted from the mid 70s to the early 90s. They were primarily designed for displaying high scores and messages, and the most famous is the Atari font. It was most likely designed by Lyle Rains for *Quiz Show* (see pages 18 and 44–45) – one of the first Atari videogames to use a microprocessor instead of discrete logic. The same font was used for most of Atari's games thereafter, and spread all over the world by other videogame developers, such as Namco, which 'adopted' it for its own titles.

The Atari font became a generic norm in the 80s videogame industry and evolved into many new variants, with modifications and stylizations. A new wave of the typeface would emerge following the rise of the Japanese videogame industry in the mid 80s. *Xevious* (see page 48) was epoch-making for its symbolic use of a bespoke sci-fi font to suit the worldview of the game. Sega used a kind of house font for games such as *Space Harrier* (see page 30) and *Fantasy Zone* (see page 56) to express their poppy, new-wave tone. Some companies developed fonts specific to individual game series, such as the thin square sans featured in the influential shoot 'em up *Gradius* (Konami, 1983).

The designers of those fonts made use of the platform's limited resolution and colours in amazing ways. You might be surprised to know that each character of those ingenious font designs was designed in 8×8 pixels, or 7×7 taking account of the single pixel space between characters. The design is not outline-based, but a composition of coloured pixels from which the illusion of letters arises.

Videogame fonts are not autonomous components like the typefaces used for printing or displaying. Videogames are bitmap-based, so consist of elemental tile patterns of pixels. All the objects, backgrounds, letters and figures are just different graphic patterns in the same system. To call them 'characters' is to construct the world of the game as typography. You may define the whole set of characters as a videogame font in the broad traditional sense. The beauty of these fonts comes from the fact that they are not substitutable.

The font is the game. We play in typography.

TOSHI OMAGARI

PREFACE

A maths teacher will tell you 8×8 equals 64, but my answer would be the infinity symbol (an eight turned on its side). In this book, you will learn why 8×8 offers infinite possibilities, at this nerdy crossroads of typography and videogames.

Typography is the centuries-old art of using selected typefaces in service of the perfect delivery of written content. Videogames are a decades-old form of entertainment that is still developing its multigenerational fanbase. What they have in common is that they are both visual media, and involve type.

Videogames have rapidly developed a unique and rich visual culture, and there is already a wealth of information available on how certain games, characters and songs were made. One aspect of this culture has so far been missing, however: the typography. I grew up with legendary games such as *Space Harrier* (Sega, 1985), and I recognize the typefaces used in those games just as easily as I do their characters. But I couldn't find a book that would take me down that particular path of videogame research.

Why is it that almost everything in videogame history has been thoroughly explored except for typography? Is it because gamers haven't found typefaces interesting, or because designers haven't yet given due credit to videogame typography for its broader impact?

It quickly became apparent that I was not alone, and there was clearly a passionate audience out there. The sensory shorthand I get from the *Space Harrier* typeface occurs in other people too, but with other classic games, such as *Shinobi* (see page 184) or *Gradius* (see page 86).

It is also true that people who do not know much about games or typefaces can still find beauty in this subject. Everyone understands letters and enjoys colours, and videogame typography requires no gaming experience to be appreciated.

I wanted to share my passion, so I started going through thousands upon thousands of arcade games, documenting the typefaces that appear in each to the best of my ability. I wrote scripts that convert the images into fully functional colour typefaces. I categorized them, examined them, and in the process learned about the whole history of arcade games, not just that of their typography.

Along the way, I found great games I had never heard of and terrible games whose typography is their saving grace. I've seen the evolution of popular games and discovered mundane typefaces that are elevated by the contexts in which they appear. I also realized that there was no book like this one, perhaps because nobody else had been crazy enough to do the necessary research.

In this book, I can only share a very small portion of the treasure trove of videogame typefaces that I found along the way. It would be impossible to be fully comprehensive, but it is enough to give you the historical context and help you to evaluate any retro typeface you may come across in the future. Most of all, I hope it inspires you to make new typefaces of your own and re-ignite the almost-lost art of pixel typography.

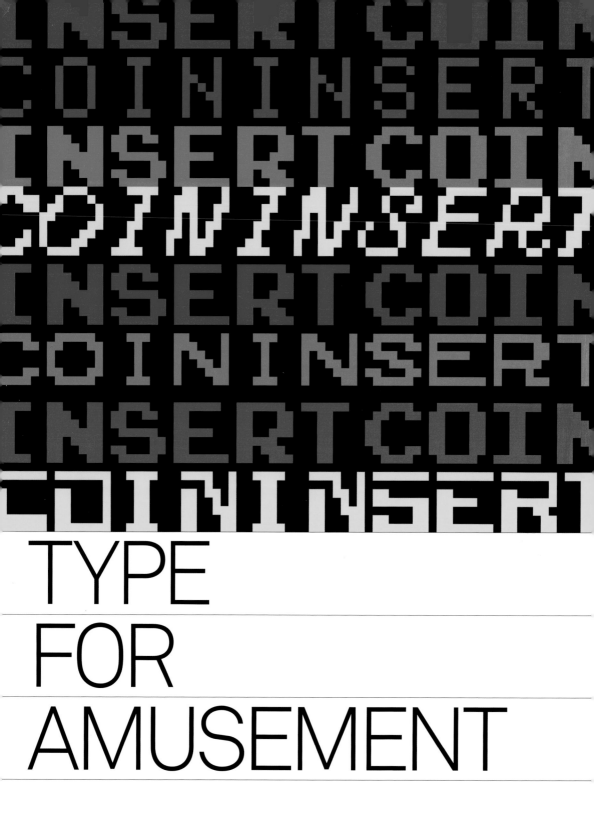

TYPE
FOR
AMUSEMENT

Videogames, as the word implies, consist primarily of digital imagery and visual feedback. Your visual experience of the game is restricted to the player characters, villains, stages and backgrounds, and that is all you seem to need on the screen.

These restrictions are, of course, limitations. Playing as a character, you cannot physically sense how hurt you are or search your pocket to see if you already have the red keycard you need. Games don't feel that real. They also have lots of special rules that do not exist in our world and need to be explained visually. These can be shown in an intuitive manner, like a health bar, but quite often rely on text.

As old-fashioned as it sounds, most games just cannot work without letters. Imagine *Pong* (Allan Alcorn, Atari, 1972) without a scoreboard. Well-executed typography immerses you in the world of the game more fully.

Typography in videogames has evolved independently to the development of professional computer typography. Videogames are a form of entertainment and this manifests itself in their typography. In arcades, a game generated coin revenue by running automatic demos, known as its 'attract mode'. Arcade cabinets were trying their hardest to appeal to teenagers and this was the case for the game fonts, too.

In the old tile-based graphics systems, you needed to make fonts from as few as 8×8 pixels. This is a tiny canvas upon which to design a typeface. Yet the majority of the fonts in this book were made in this format, adding up to nearly 1,600 unique families through the use of multiple colours and animations. It is fascinating to see how much can be squeezed out of this small format.

Limitation is a great driver of creativity, as is technological innocence. Game developers could not install commercial fonts on low-bit arcade cabinets with raster graphics, and anyway it was far cheaper to draw their own. The lack of commercial interest in, and influence from, the computer type industry has resulted in a collection of beautiful art created by outsiders. Japan was the most dominant force in the early gaming industry and many of its game developers were unfamiliar with the Latin alphabet. They were not always thorough when it came to translating their games into English, as may be seen in unintentionally funny mistranslations, such as 'all your base are belong to us' in *Zero Wing* (Toaplan, 1989). The developers' lack of everyday exposure to the language and its alphabet is also evident in the typeface designs. You will discover a number of baffling oddities in this book that are better explained as products of naivety than creativity.

Even a good typeface can 'suffer' if it is not suited for the game in which it is featured, which you will discover is a common occurrence in early videogame typography. For example, featuring a flowing script-like typeface in a space shoot 'em up (see page 179) is not 'wrong', but it is far from conventional and enriches our understanding of the cultural differences at play in the nascent arcade industry.

In type design for print, it is often said that 'good typography is invisible'. This can also be the case in typography for videogames, with legible, at-a-glance information on health, lives and remaining playtime empowering the player on an almost subconscious level – critical in games like versus fighters, where fractions of seconds count. But it is perhaps when pixel type stands apart from conventional typography and indulges its own quirks, such as graduating colours or animation, that it comes into its own, a vital part of the sensory bombardment of early arcade videogames.

This book covers roughly three decades
of arcade-game history, showcasing typefaces
from hit titles, unsung gems and abject failures.
Although typography for 8- and 16-bit videogames
takes many forms, to provide a focused survey
I restricted my research to the most common
character set: the 8×8 pixel format.

In the history of videogames, the arcade game presents a new brand of entertainment in its earliest form. If you wanted to see the newest, most exciting visuals, you would always go to the arcades. Even then, counting variants, revisions and bootlegs, there are more than 7,000 games to consider. In the course of researching this book, I have reviewed around 4,500 games.

The graphical format of videogames is a self-imposed limitation. The classical definition of a font is that it is formed of a full set of letters that are available to be keyed in any combination. By this definition, title logos do not count, since they are locked graphics with letters that are not supposed to be reused to form other words. The 8×8 format is another key limitation of arcade-game type. There are a variety of sizes of typeface available in videogames, in different multiples of eight – 8×8, 8×16 or 32×32 – but 8×8 imposes the strictest graphical constraints, making it the most interesting to study.

As a general rule, most typefaces included in the book have a full set of twenty-six uppercase or lowercase letters as a minimum. There are, however, a few exceptions to this rule, and some character sets are not shown in full. Since the letters and numerals are usually the only common characters across all the featured fonts, the presentation of the fonts in this book is mainly limited to letters, diacritics and numerals,

although dollar signs and other symbols have been shown in some places for interest.

Some fonts might look different against a white background, but it's worth remembering that they were not intended to be shown this way. Each game has its own background colours. Earlier games were typically black, but later releases had a constantly changing palette, from skies to forests, and even nude women. The colour schemes, or palettes, were often available in multiple variations for each game. Here you will see one palette for each typeface, but keep in mind that there may be more. If a typeface does not have multiple colours in its design, it is shown here in black, regardless of its colour in its game.

Keeping things simple

As I imagine most readers belong to either the gaming or design worlds, and rarely both, I have used simplified terms in the service of gaming readers who know less about typography and vice versa.

As a type enthusiast, I must make a disclaimer about the difference between a typeface and a font. A typeface is an abstract idea, a design that does not take any physical form, while a font is the physical manifestation of a typeface. Traditionally, different sizes were separate fonts; metal type could not be scaled, and you had to have each size in your printing inventory. If you have Times New Roman in 6pt metal, 12pt metal, and digital OpenType

1

CREDITS: 0

1 CREDIT / 1 COIN

2 CREDITS TO START.
2 CREDITS TO CONTINUE.

INSERT COIN

화성암 조직의 큰 결정들 사이에 있는
작은 알갱이를 무엇이라 하나?

중화기
무 기
석 기
백 기

LIFE 1P   2P LIFE

format, then you have one typeface in three fonts. Today, people say 'font' to mean 'typeface', and I also use them interchangeably in this book.

The typeface classification in this book does not strictly follow convention – I have made my own, so that it makes more sense here. 'Sans' is quite a large group, and subdivided into three smaller groups depending on the weight. 'Serif' contains all weight variations. 'MICR', discussed in detail later, is its own category due to its popularity. 'Slanted' is separate from 'Calligraphy & Lettering' – typefaces with handwritten flavour have been

placed in 'Calligraphy & Lettering' – as a combined category would be too broad, although the differences can be very subtle.

'Horizontal Stress' contains any typeface whose horizontal strokes are thicker than verticals, regardless of the base style.

'Stencil' is home to designs that look like they have been stencilled, but also those that look like stencils.

'Decorative' is for everything else, or any design whose decoration is the most important part.

These distinctions are sometimes flimsy and fonts can sit across categories.

There are very few named type designers in this book, as it is rare

to find them in game credit rolls. Japanese game companies had a practice of not listing real names in their credit rolls, fearing their employees would be headhunted by competitors. This means it is often very difficult to definitively identify the people involved in the creation of a typeface.

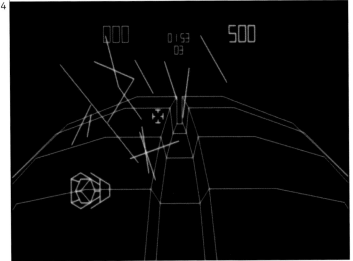

The following types of game are not included for different reasons:
1. Not on arcade (e.g. *Sonic the Hedgehog 2*, Sega, 1992).
2. Not monospaced (e.g. *Mortal Kombat*, Midway, 1992).
3. Larger than 8×8, and not Latin (e.g. *Date Quiz Go Go Episode 2*, SemiCom, 2000).
4. Vector-scan format (e.g. *Starhawk*, Cinematronics, 1979).

THE 8×8 MONOSPACED

Videogames are ruled by multiples of two. Binaries and bits are the currency of the gaming world and everything on the screen was once composed of 'tiles', with each tile made up of multiples of two. You can find 4×4 pixel tiles, and 8×16, moving up to 32×32 and higher in the 90s, but the most common unit was 8×8. This was the case at least until 3D graphics became dominant in the late 90s to early 00s.

What is the smallest number of pixels you need to make all the capital letters and numbers, but which is also easy for a computer to process? The most complex characters are B, E and S, plus 2, 3, 5, 6, 8 and 9 – all of which can be drawn at an absolute minimum of five pixels high.

In the horizontal dimension, each Latin letter varies in width, and ideally any new font should try to replicate this variability, but programming width variance is a costly calculation. Why use a wider character that fills up more space? Monospaced fonts, with identical character widths, were therefore considered satisfactory for videogames, due in part to the fact that most games were made in Japan, where the writing system is also primarily monospaced.*

An 8×8-pixel tile is the second smallest set of multiples of two, but even this slightly larger size is restrictive in terms of the number of pixels that can be used. Tiles are displayed side by side, horizontally and vertically, with no gaps in between. This means that any letter spacing has to be included in the tile. If you drew your capital M in full eight-pixel width and typed MMM, the letters would join together and become illegible. This limits you to seven pixels to design with, at most, in either direction – the last row of pixels must function as a space.

Most game typefaces use the 8×8-pixel grid to the fullest by saving the outermost pixel rows for outlines or drop shadows, which then function naturally as spaces and also help the font to stand out against a busy background. When multicoloured type design became commonplace in the early 80s, these became very popular styles of decoration.

Colour is something that traditional type designers do not usually deal with, because type colouring is done at the graphic design level, not at the font creation level. For a font designer, monospaced 8×8-pixel blocks may at first appear too restrictive to allow for diversity, until they discover that by using multiple colours in varied ways they can create an entire universe of distinctive designs. Videogames are entertainment and so their fonts are commercially incentivized to appear as flashy as possible when compared to older computer fonts, which just needed to work.

Eight pixels sounds tiny by the standards of today. Screen pixel counts have improved significantly and we now have mobile-phone screens that display over 400 pixels per inch. At the same resolution, eight pixels appear smaller than half a millimetre. Old games on cathode-ray tube (CRT) displays had lower resolutions, of course, and eight pixels appeared larger, but exactly how large? If eight-pixel

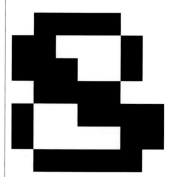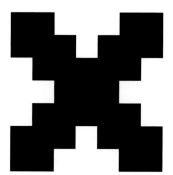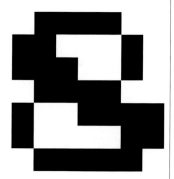

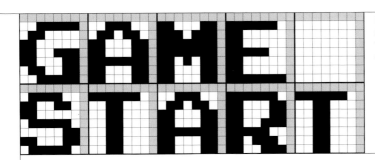

Here, the spacing pixels have been coloured grey so they stand out from the black and white pixels of the 7×7 character grid.

fonts remained popular for over two decades, was that because they were the most legible option, or because nobody tried to improve upon them?

The internal resolution of videogames did not really change until the mid 90s, which also coincided with the end of the 16-bit console era. Until then, common resolutions were approximately 300 pixels horizontally and in the low 200s vertically, such as 288×224 or 320×240. Resolutions such as 480×360 started to become common only in the 3D era, and so there are not many pixel-based games that are available at these higher resolutions.

Secondly, arcade cabinets generally had 19-inch CRT displays, which, in a 4:3 aspect ratio, are 289.56 mm high (assuming internal vertical resolution at 224 pixels). The physical size of eight pixels was therefore 10.34 mm, a reasonably legible size at a short distance that

also allowed for plenty of creative designs. It was as if the format naturally guaranteed legibility.

As there are so many monospaced fonts in this book, you may deduce that all arcade-game fonts were of this type and that videogames could not handle proportionally spaced fonts. This is not true at all, and companies such as Williams and Midway had developed their own proportional typesetting systems at an earlier stage.

There is a technical reason I could not investigate Williams and Midway games more fully. There was a completely different kind of technology in the early arcade that employed vector graphics instead of pixels, meaning game screens were filled with sharp, colourful straight lines, but no curves. Not only do such fonts pose a technical challenge to collect and analyse, but their lack of weight variation and curves limits their diversity. Games such

as Atari's *Tempest* (1981) and all of Cinematronics' games are therefore omitted here, but there are some interesting font examples in this category if you care to look into these further.

---

*This is a tradition solidified by typesetting, and *hiragan*. Historically, Japanese syllabic writing was not monospaced in handwriting. Even today, many digital Japanese fonts come equipped with proportional options.

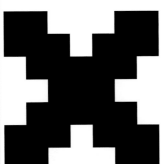
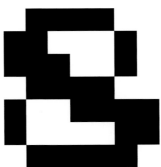
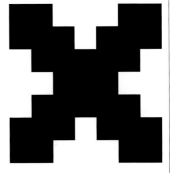

01

SANS REGULAR

OOOO   OOOO

DUNCE

GAME OVER

THE KEE GAMES QUIZ SHOW

25 CENTS PER PLAYER

TEST YOUR KNOWLEDGE \

TEST A FRIEND\S \

ABCDEFGHIJKLM
NOPQRSTUVWXYZ
0123456789

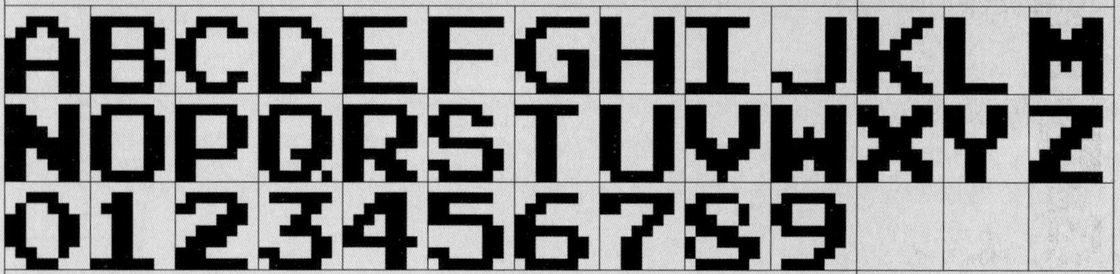

QUIZ SHOW KEE GAMES/ATARI/1976

The first appearance of this legendary typeface seems to be in *Quiz Show* (see also pages 44–45). The game cabinet had two sets of four buttons for two players, and six coloured tapes to make the black and white screen look colourful (the effect has been recreated in the screenshot above). The font also includes a black square and diagonal lines at different angles, as well as arrows in four directions.

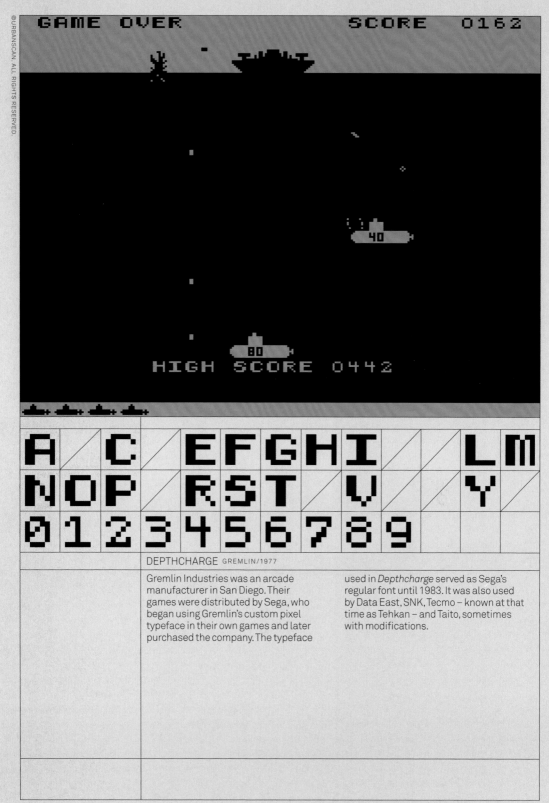

GAME OVER   SCORE   0162

HIGH SCORE 0442

DEPTHCHARGE GREMLIN/1977

Gremlin Industries was an arcade manufacturer in San Diego. Their games were distributed by Sega, who began using Gremlin's custom pixel typeface in their own games and later purchased the company. The typeface used in *Depthcharge* served as Sega's regular font until 1983. It was also used by Data East, SNK, Tecmo – known at that time as Tehkan – and Taito, sometimes with modifications.

GEE BEE NAMCO/1978

The typeface in *Gee Bee* marked the first use of Quiz Show by Namco (see pages 18 and 44–45). This version has several modifications: E's bottom bar is a pixel shorter, and the letter is aligned to the right, along with the rest of the characters.

Y has a stronger corner on the right, which may or may not be a mistake. The following year an almost identical typeface was used in *Bomb Bee* (Namco, 1979), except that a single pixel had been removed from the Y to make it symmetrical.

BASKETBALL ATARI/1978

Atari also began to modify Quiz Show, as seen here in *Basketball*. The E's bottom bar is shortened, but not re-spaced as in Gee Bee. The J has a square ending, S is equally proportioned, and 0 does not have

a diagonal stress. This particular design did not thrive, but its modifications, save for J, would be seen in other Quiz Show variants. *Missile Command* (Atari, 1980) used it, for example, but with the original J.

GALAXIAN NAMCO/1979

Galaxian, Namco's flashy take on *Space Invaders* (see page 84), was famous for the 'power-up' trick players could perform when kidnapped by a certain enemy. Released five months after *Bomb Bee*, its font is almost identical –

the only difference being that the capital Y is more in line with the character of W. Galaxian became a popular typeface in its own right, appearing in nearly 200 games including *Donkey Kong* (Nintendo, 1981).

01 SANS REGULAR

HIGHWAY CHASE DATA EAST/1980

Highway Chase is the first game to showcase the full uppercase alphabet of Depthcharge (see page 19). The letter height is six pixels, not seven, a thick stroke is applied only once per letter, and the waist is high (with the exception of A, G, P and Y). The J is thicker and Z, descending by a pixel, is thinner. The numerals do not match the letters.

CHEEKY MOUSE UNIVERSAL/1980

Cheeky Mouse was created by Japanese manufacturer Universal, which is not the Hollywood film studio. The typeface was made especially for the game but it seems to be a questionable choice for the pest-control theme – it would, perhaps, better suit a mechanical sci-fi setting. The style is driven by the slanting A and lowercase-like M and N. The M and W use the full width of the pixel grid and 0 misses a pixel – mistakes that were corrected in the next iteration of the typeface that appears in *Zero Hour* (Universal, 1980).

QUASAR ZELCO/ZACCARIA/1980

Zaccaria was a pinball and arcade manufacturer from Bologna, Italy, which created a uniform typeface for use across all of its games. First appearing in *Galaxia* (Zaccaria, 1979) with an incomplete character set, the typeface was completed in *Quasar*. It is not a very consistent design: B looks large, J's top serif is oversized, and the character looks smaller than I. S is blocky, and 3 and 8 are too narrow.

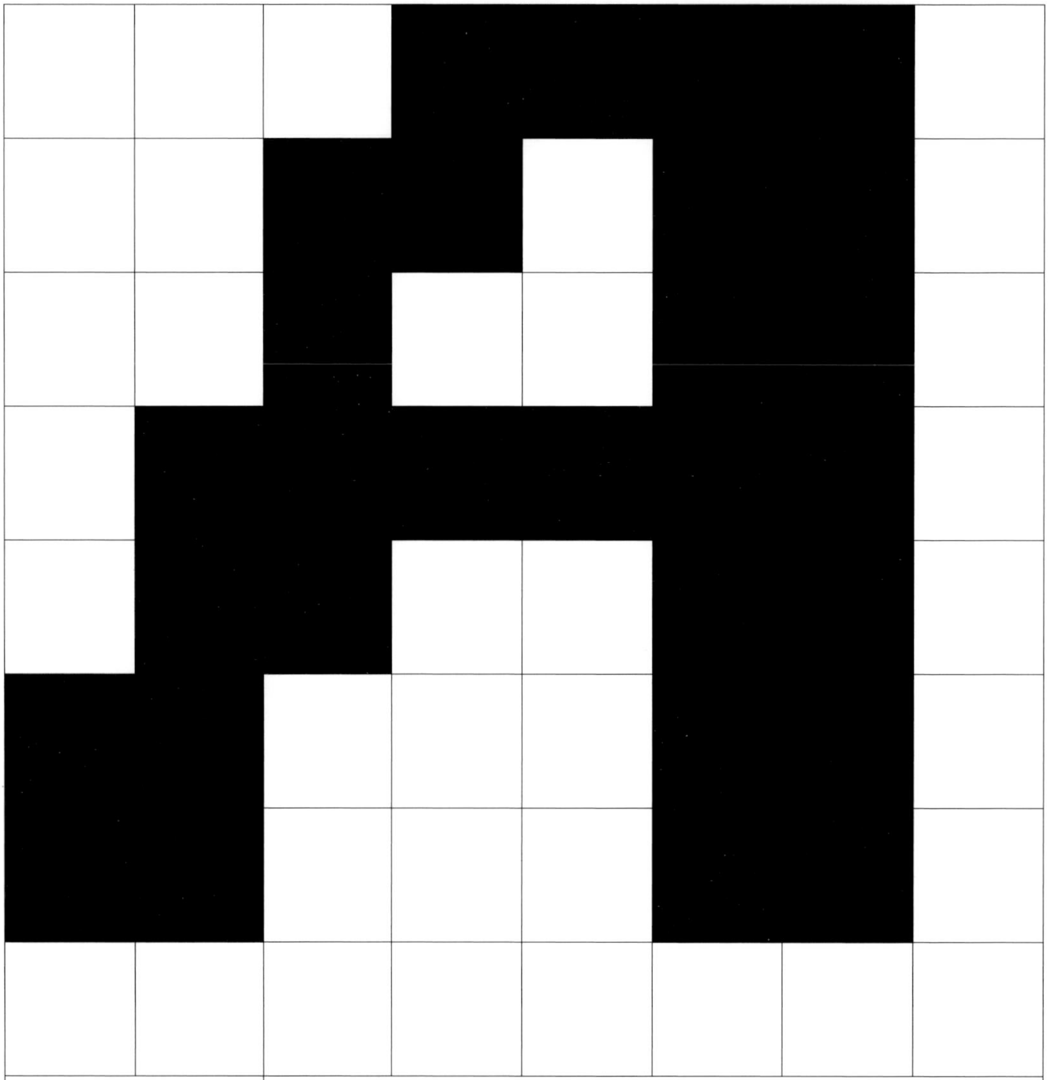

CHEEKY MOUSE
UNIVERSAL/1980

01 SANS REGULAR

ROC'N ROPE
KONAMI/1983

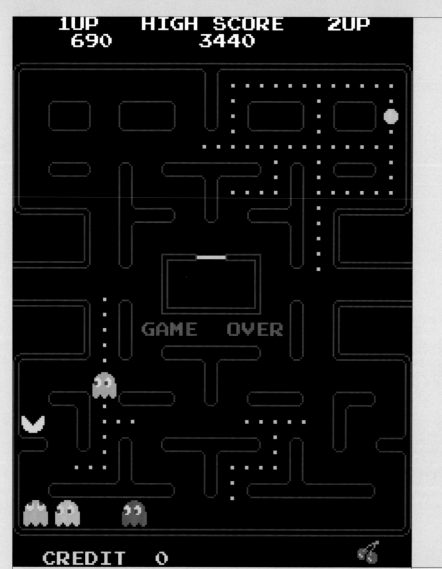

PAC-MAN NAMCO/1980

Pac-Man's typeface is essentially Gee Bee (see page 20), but with a symmetrical Y. When documenting the development of a typeface over time, details like this must be taken seriously. *Pac-Man* is an especially important example as it used the most popular variant of the Atari font, primarily used by Namco but appearing elsewhere too, thanks to the popularity of the game. *Shovel Knight* (Yacht Club Games, 2014) uses the *Pac-Man* typeface, with a widened E.

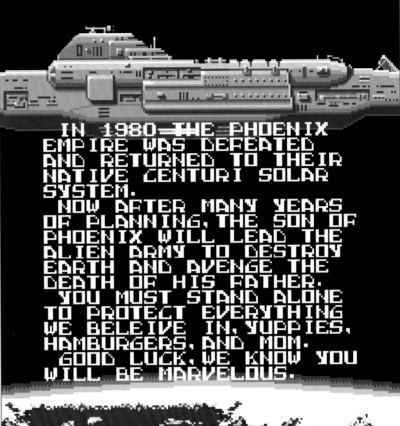

IN 1980 THE PHOENIX
EMPIRE WAS DEFEATED
AND RETURNED TO THEIR
NATIVE CENTURI SOLAR
SYSTEM.
   NOW AFTER MANY YEARS
OF PLANNING,THE SON OF
PHOENIX WILL LEAD THE
ALIEN ARMY TO DESTROY
EARTH AND AVENGE THE
DEATH OF HIS FATHER.
   YOU MUST STAND ALONE
TO PROTECT EVERYTHING
WE BELEIVE IN,YUPPIES,
HAMBURGERS,AND MOM.
   GOOD LUCK,WE KNOW YOU
WILL BE MARVELOUS.

ABCDEFGHIJKLM
NOPQRSTUVWXYZ
0123456789

SON OF PHOENIX ASSOCIATED OVERSEAS MFR, INC/1985

The typeface for *Son of Phoenix* makes liberal use of 45° strokes and round shapes squared off at the bottom. It has a mechanical and futuristic feel, but it isn't wholly cohesive. The real reason for including this typeface here is to show the game's delightful opening sequence. Unlike the famous 'All your base...' (see page 11), the phrase 'yuppies, hamburgers and mom' is not the result of a bad English translation – it doesn't make any sense in Japanese either.

ABCDEFGHIJKLM
NOPQRSTUVWXYZ
0123456789

MONSTER BASH SEGA/1982

Monster Bash is identical to Galaxian (see page 20). The typeface is coloured red with a black drop shadow, which is fitting for a horror game. Monster Bash marks the beginnings of multicoloured makeovers of the Quiz Show (see pages 18 and 44–45) branch of videogame typography.

ABCDEFGHIJKLM
NOPQRSTUVWXYZ
0123456789

GYRUSS KONAMI/1983

Gyruss is a 3D cylinder shooter, clearly influenced by *Tempest* (Atari, 1981). This second appearance of multicoloured Quiz Show uses the *Pac-Man* variant (see page 24) coloured in three diagonally separated layers.

ABCDEFGHIJKLM
NOPQRSTUVWXYZ
abcdefghijklm
nopqrstuvwxyz
0123456789

ROC'N ROPE KONAMI/1983

In *Roc'n Rope*, the player becomes an adventurer armed with a grappling hook and on the hunt for a phoenix. The typeface is based on Quiz Show, but all of the changes in this version have worsened the overall effectiveness of the font. The attempt to make Quiz Show lowercase has created new characters that do not cohere visually with the design of the capitals, and are not used in the game.

PHOZON NAMCO/1983

The typeface created for *Phozon* was Namco's attempt at making Quiz Show lowercase, and it was the most harmonious version at the time. The uppercase is also new, narrowing E and F, and sharpening the bottom of W.

The lowercase design has long ascenders and in- and out-strokes in letters like a and n, while g is faithful to the typographic two-storey form. The ascending g became a common compromise in videogame type design.

MARBLE MADNESS ATARI GAMES/1984

In *Marble Madness*, you can see Atari's take on a lowercase version of Quiz Show. It has fewer decorative elements, so better resembles the uppercase than any other design up until this point. It also utilizes

anti-aliasing, a colour-blending technique applied to certain pixels to create the illusion of smooth edges. The technique has been applied to S, r, s and w, but it is too modest to be effective.

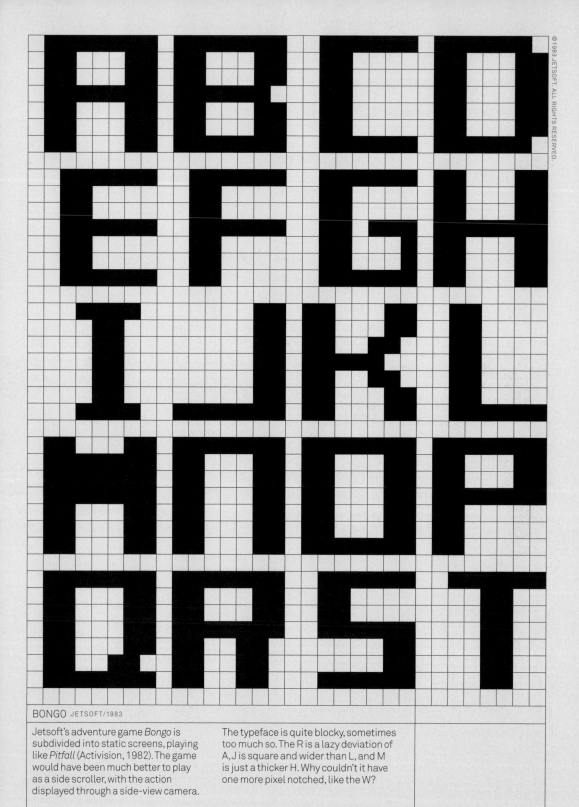

BONGO JETSOFT/1983

Jetsoft's adventure game *Bongo* is subdivided into static screens, playing like *Pitfall* (Activision, 1982). The game would have been much better to play as a side scroller, with the action displayed through a side-view camera.

The typeface is quite blocky, sometimes too much so. The R is a lazy deviation of A, J is square and wider than L, and M is just a thicker H. Why couldn't it have one more pixel notched, like the W?

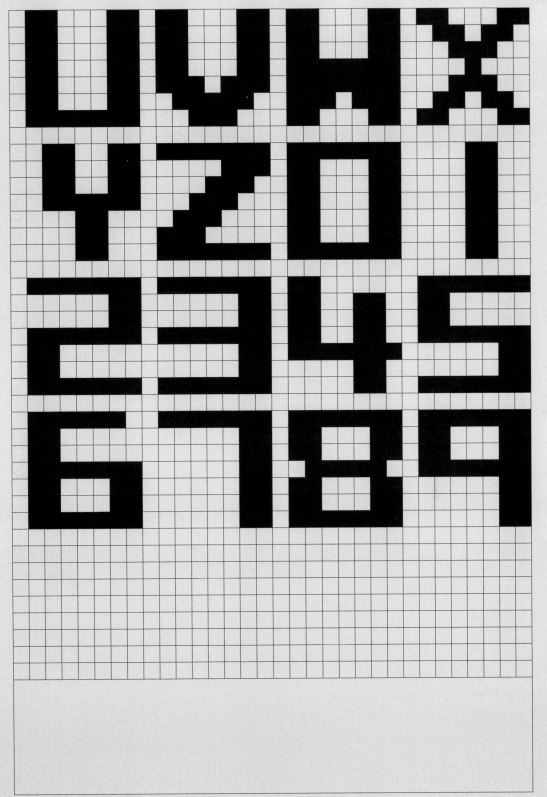

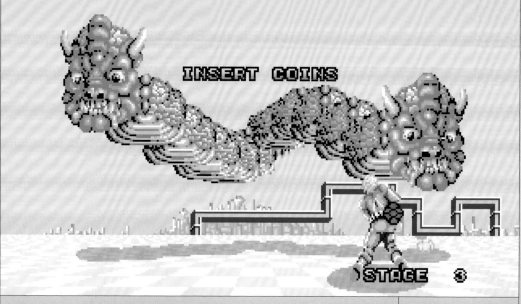

SPACE HARRIER SEGA/1985

Sega's creativity exploded in 1985. The base letterform design used in *Space Harrier* is a return to Depthcharge (see page 19) with a twist – a notable change to the serif of F. Unfortunately, the V looks as if it has been accidentally scrolled down by a pixel. The typeface was first designed for *Hang-On* five months earlier, which had no gradient and a correctly drawn V.

LEGEND CORELAND/SEGA/1986

In *Legend*, a country is in peril and the hero of the game must throw bags of dollars at his enemies to bribe them into changing sides. The bold colours used in the typeface are perhaps meant to evoke the American flag, an appropriate palette for this game. It also lacks a lowercase character set; now that is what I call capitalism.

HOT CHASE KONAMI/1988

A racing game in which your car has timed explosives on board – it's basically Sega's *Out Run* (see page 219) with angry people shooting at you. The square and strict 45°-angled strokes of the typeface recall those used in Konami's own game *Gradius* (see page 86), but here the characters are two pixels thick horizontally, and the round letters are less harsh on the eye. The number of colours on the high-score screen is especially delightful.

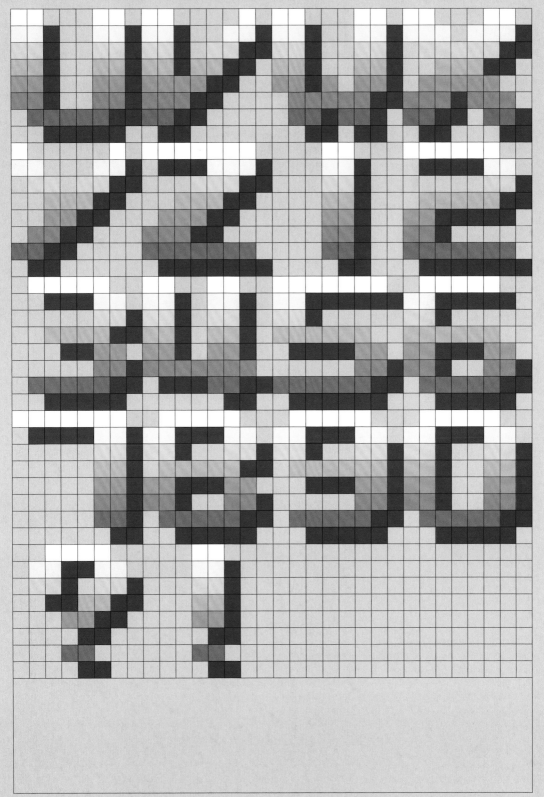

SNEZHNAJA KOROLEVA — TERMINAL / 1988

An exception to the rule of sticking to the Latin alphabet, *Snezhnaja Koroleva*, meaning 'snow queen', is a maze-runner game based on a 1957 Russian cartoon of the same name. Designed by arcade developer Terminal, this typeface has many quirky features. Ň's breve is expressed in a single pixel, and the designers have repurposed the character ч as a 4. The D and F, although not part of the Cyrillic alphabet, may have been necessary technical additions to the typeface in order to display hexadecimal numbers for debugging.

TEENAGE MUTANT NINJA TURTLES — KONAMI / 1989

The pastel tone above instantly brings to mind a fondly remembered game from the 90s – *Teenage Mutant Ninja Turtles*. The basic structure of this typeface is standard, but the use of a mid-tone colour to anti-alias the edges is not quite successful. C and S look thinner than the other letters, for example. On the other hand, V could have benefited from a thinner stroke on the right. V is also the only asymmetric character, and seems to have come from *Gradius* (see page 86).

GAIN GROUND — SEGA / 1988

Gain Ground was a strategic shooter game heavily inspired by Atari's *Gauntlet* (1985), according to its developer. The gameplay involves more planning and foresight than quick reactions to incoming attacks. The typography mainly consisted of larger fonts in uncial style and this font is a reduced version. Although Gain Ground is aiming for a calligraphic aesthetic, the end result is closer to a sans serif with occasional eye-catching details like those seen in A, B, N, Q and U. The white pixel at the top left is a quick and easy recreation of the 3D emboss effect that is present in larger versions of the typeface.

01 SANS REGULAR

DYNAMITE DUKE SEIBU KAIHATSU/1989

A gallery shooter with a mobile protagonist that inspired *Wild Guns* (Natsume, 1994). *Dynamite Duke*'s typeface is a beautifully minimal yet stylized square sans, with corners at top right and bottom left where possible. The numerals are taller, with a military look, which sits in stark contrast with the capitals. Despite the bold differences between the characters, the letters and numbers were indeed used together.

MICHAEL JACKSON'S MOONWALKER SEGA/1990

Michael Jackson was a big fan of videogames, especially those from Sega. The Mega Drive and arcade versions of *Moonwalker* are completely different in almost every aspect except the story, as the latter is more of a beat 'em up, and allows up to three Michaels to play together. The typeface is also different, as each letter has the top left trimmed, apart from the iconic capital M.

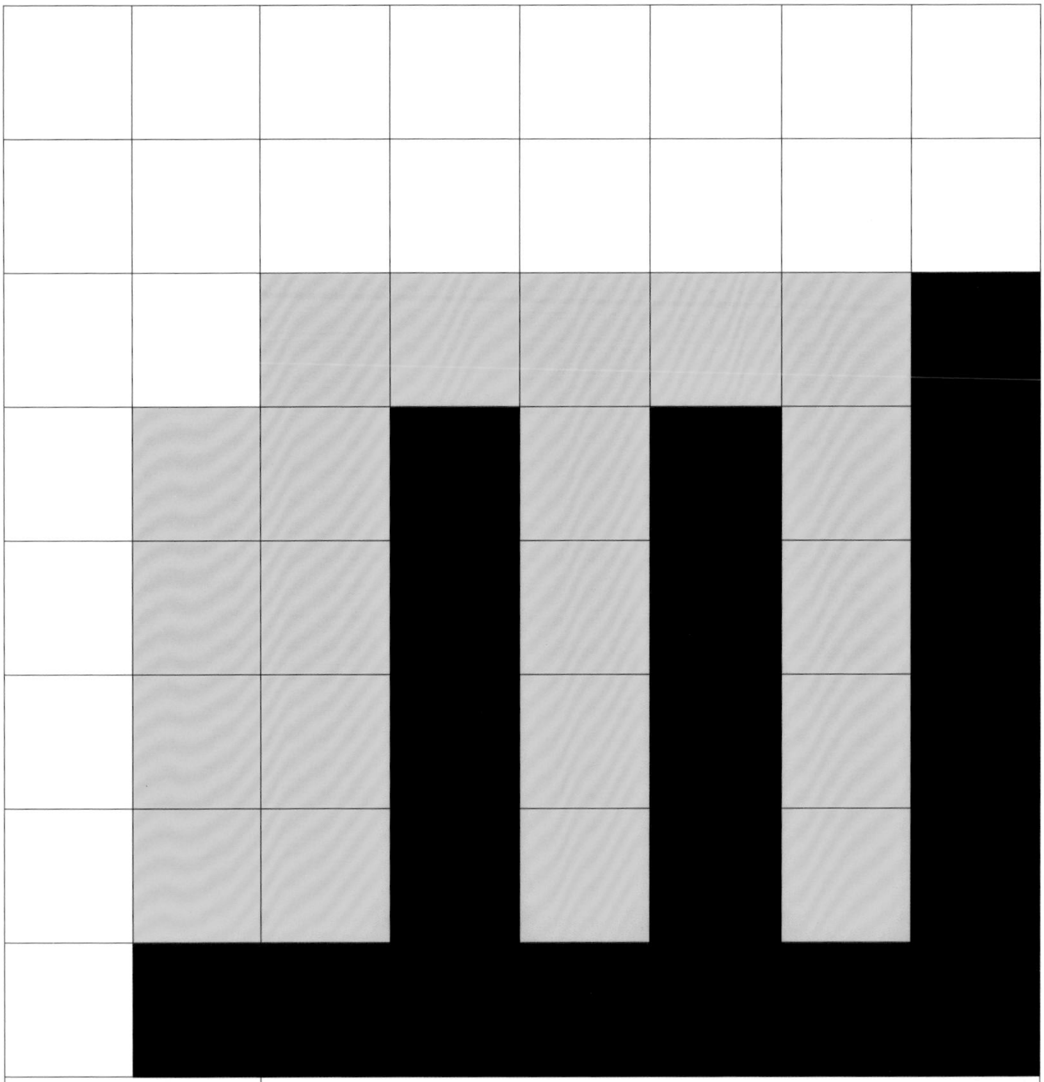

MICHAEL JACKSON'S
MOONWALKER
SEGA/1990

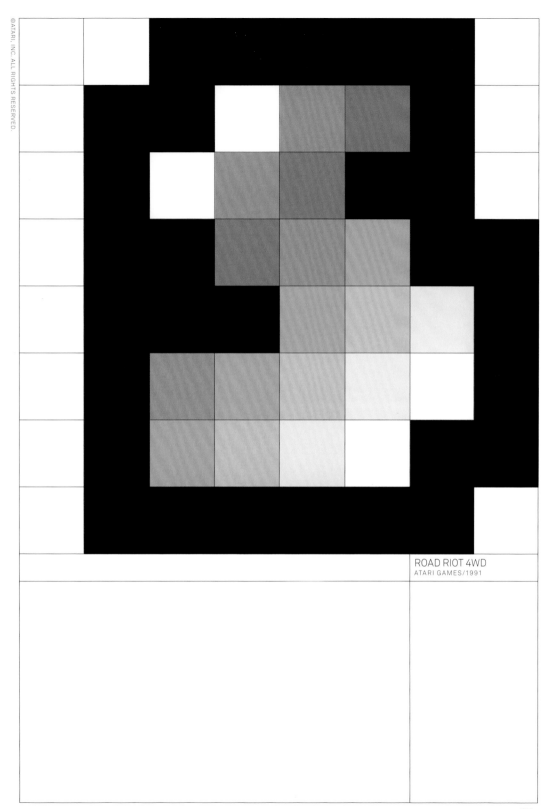

ROAD RIOT 4WD
ATARI GAMES/1991

ROAD RIOT 4WD ATARI/1991

The typeface for this game, in which the player races a dune buggy against three armed opponents, is a rather metallic outlined font with a lowercase based on Colin Brignall's 1968 Letraset typeface Revue. The game also had a 16×16 capital font that was basically Helvetica, and these 8×8 caps seem to echo those forms. The unified lowercase looks nice, but some letters look tiny on the screen. Atari had adapted Revue the previous year in *Hydra* (see page 254).

VIRTUA RACING SEGA/1992

Virtua Racing was a technical demo for Sega's Model 1 board. It was well received, so the company decided to make it into a proper game. This typeface does not appear in the game (except in the Mega Drive port), but is used as the system font for the Model 1. The lowercase is missing ascenders and descenders.

NAMCO CLASSICS COLLECTION VOL.1 NAMCO/1995

Namco originally made this typeface for a vertical shoot 'em up called *NebulasRay* in 1994, then added a set of lowercase characters the next year. The height setting, letter proportion and colouring are very similar to Dynamite Duke (see page 35), but less stylized. The lowercase is nicely done for the most part – except for the unnecessarily low j and descending e, which are disappointing, since the designers crammed s into the same 4-pixel x-height.

VIRTUA FIGHTER REMIX SEGA/1995

Virtua Fighter was released in 1993. It was the first 3D fighting game and revolutionized the industry. *Remix* was released after *Virtua Fighter 2* as a graphical update of the original, which now supported textures. This typeface is similar to that used for the Sega Model 1 console. However, the designers have used partial shadows here instead of a complete outline, allowing for extra pixels and creating space for M and W. The lowercase height is now lower, also. It doesn't seem to be used in the arcade, but does appear in the Sega Saturn version.

MVP SEGA/1989

A baseball game with a comical art style. The gameplay was good for its time, but is not particularly noteworthy today. For no apparent reason, the typefaces used in the game generally have a gelatinous texture, but they do look good.

This typeface has that effect, and it's an example of a simple idea executed well. The outline logic is inconsistent (see O, for example), but it's not bad enough to break the design.

GAIAPOLIS KONAMI/1993

A vertical beat 'em up with RPG elements, set in a fantasy steampunk future. The game is just as awesome as it sounds, but was totally buried in the fighting game craze back in the day. The typeface is an adaptation of Brignall's Revue without the slits, and the grey palette fits the pastel tone of the game. The outline is only partial, and you can also see it as a shadow effect.

MOUJA ETONA/1996

A familiarity with Japanese coins is essential to the gameplay and the levels of difficulty in *Mouja*, so this puzzle-game series, which started in Windows 3.1, remained exclusive to Japan. The typeface above was designed for the arcade version of the game. It features square yet somehow rounded capitals and numbers, and more diagonal, serif-like lowercase lettering. See the semi-slanted 9 and squashed g.

PLAYER1 00128000 AREA ZONE AREA
MISSILE BOMB ARM A & B
×2

INSERT COIN(S)

CAPTURE BALL

CREDIT 0

ABCDEFGHIJKLM
NOPQRSTUVWXYZ
αβγδεζηθικλμν
ξοπ123456789

G-DARIUS TAITO/1997

Taito was another big fan of the *Pac-Man* typeface (see page 24) and the *Darius* series had a 16×16 pixel version. The *G-Darius* team then went on to make a standard sans with a simple yet effective emboss. *Darius* was a series known for its branching storylines, a type of nonlinear gameplay, with each narrative named alphabetically, and *G-Darius* used Greek lowercase. Hence, we have a rare occasion of Greek in this collection, though only up to omicron. A good Greek type is a very tall order, but this is a noble effort.

THE ATARI FONT

Of all the arcade-game typefaces, none is as dominant or iconic as that designed by Atari. If any font deserves its own chapter, it is this one, which has become visual shorthand for the pre-3D gaming era. Although it does not have an official name, it is commonly known as the Atari font, Namco font or simply as 'arcade font'. Before examining the typeface in more detail, however, we must indulge in a detective story.

The Atari font first appeared in 1976 in *Sprint 2* and *Cannonball* by Kee Games, an Atari subsidiary. There has been some debate over the very first appearance, but it's generally believed to be the former title. The game was made by Lyle Rains and Dennis Koble and, according to the accounts of former employees at Kee Games, the typeface was designed by Rains.

Cannonball was made by Owen Rubin, who was a new employee at Kee Games. He made the graphics for the game, but does not recall making the typeface himself: 'I am fairly sure that Lyle made the font for *Sprint 2* and, if the *Cannonball* font is the same, I suspect I used his font in *Cannonball*, or at least copied it'. He also said Koble joined the company after him, which may place *Sprint 2* after *Cannonball*, making it harder still to figure out the chronology.

It was very recently discovered, however, that Kee Games also released another game in 1976, called *Quiz Show* (see pages 18 and 44–45), which used the same typeface, so there are in fact three possible origins, rather than two. *Quiz Show* is the most likely for three reasons. First, at that time arcade fonts could be incomplete, as they only had to support the minimum set of letters used in the game (high-scores tables did not yet exist). However, text-based games like *Quiz Show*

needed to have fully-fledged fonts. Secondly, the dates of the service manuals for *Quiz Show* and *Sprint 2* indicate that the former was released in April, six months before the latter.* Rubin's recollection tallies with this: 'I believe *Quiz Show* was released before Dennis or I even started. It was most likely done by Lyle'. Finally, *Quiz Show*, *Sprint 2* and *Cannonball* were the first games to be made for the processor-based system, and the level of graphical detail required to create the Atari font was just not possible prior to this point.

Digital cutting edge

The exact circumstances of the font's creation are not fully known, but we have a fairly clear idea of its production method.

At that time, every game graphic was made on graph paper, and then the artwork was coded by hand, one pixel at a time. The Atari font was most likely designed in this way. We must not forget that this was long before fully digital design processes emerged: MacPaint came to Macintosh in 1984, and Photoshop arrived in 1990. For a good proportion of gaming history, font-making was carried out by graphic artists with or without lettering experience, or sometimes even by the game's programmers.

Quiz Show was the first typeface to be two pixels thick vertically and one pixel horizontally, with

a 45°-diagonal 'roundness' that made D and O more distinguishable. Its identifying features are the E with its horizontal bars at three different lengths, the S with a thin spine and a leftward lean, and 0 and 8 with a diagonal stroke contrast that helps to distinguish them from similar-looking letters. S, 3 and 8 are narrower on top, unlike B or G.

Atari went on using the font in their games, but Namco, which became Atari's Japanese distributor after acquiring Atari Japan, was arguably more influential in popularizing the typeface. Namco started releasing its own games and used Quiz Show, possibly because it was simply the most recognizable font at the time.

Typography was not a high priority for game designers, especially when it came to working with an unfamiliar writing system (the Latin alphabet), so using a design created by native English speakers was a safer choice than designing something new from scratch. Quiz Show was first used by Namco in *Bomb Bee* and *Cutie Q* (both 1979), the latter of which also used another classic typeface from Atari's *Tank 8* (see page 83).

Namco used Quiz Show in all of its 1980 releases, but the game that really made the font's name was *Pac-Man* (1980, see page 24). The font design spread among

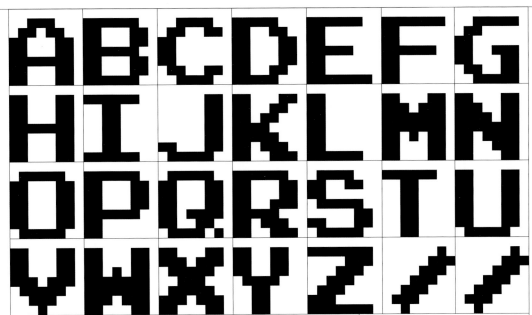

other Japanese developers too: Nintendo used it in numerous arcade and console games, such as *Donkey Kong* (1982), *Duck Hunt* (1984), *Super Mario Bros.* (1985) and *The Legend of Zelda* (1986).

Namco had several different design variations originating either in *Galaxian* (1979, see page 20) or *Pac-Man*, but the latter variant became the most popular and remained so until the end of the PlayStation era. Because of this, Quiz Show, or the *Pac-Man* variant, is primarily known in Japan as the Namco font.

The show's not over

As arcade components became more powerful and game developers got more creative with graphics, the Quiz Show typeface in its original form gradually lost its popularity, as its use in games was seen to represent a lack of creativity.

Facing tough competition against ever-increasing options, Quiz Show's appearance continued to diversify, especially in terms of its decorations, such as shadows and gradients. An abundance of weights, colours and decorative

variants make the Atari font a category all of its own.

In the post-arcade videogame era, the typeface regained its place as the go-to videogame font, instantly evocative of coin-op's pop-cultural status. It is used in all kinds of gaming-related graphics and pseudo-retro games, such as *Shovel Knight* (Yacht Club Games, 2014), which, judging by its design, appears to use a later version of the *Pac-Man* variant.

This font's ubiquity is justified by its bold, utilitarian, neutral appearance. Adopted across the industry and constantly evolving, its influence is undeniable. It's a typeface that forgot to become obsolete – the Helvetica of videogame fonts.

* Judging by the lack of marketing materials or existing cabinets, *Cannonball* probably did not move past the prototype stage.

Quiz Show's 8×8-pixel grid is small compared to other formats – Midway favoured 8×16 – and it has some quirks and inconsistencies, but remains legible.

02

SANS BOLD

ABCDEFGHIJKLM
NOPQRSTUVWXYZ
0123456789

GRAND CHAMPION TAITO/1981

A top-view racing game that features changing weather conditions such as rain and snow. Taito stopped using Atari fonts and started making its own typefaces around 1980 and this is among the first.

It is a very nice sans, and the numerals are perfect. However, K could have been thicker, and X has an unsightly extra pixel that was removed in later Taito games.

ABCDEFGHIJKLM
NOPQRSTUVWXYZ
0123456789

LOCO-MOTION KONAMI/1982

The tiles in this sliding puzzle are train rails, and the goal is to guide a moving locomotive to the exit. The typeface for the game is most likely based on the Art Deco typeface Broadway (Morris Fuller Benton, 1927), and only a few letters are

noticeably different, such as M and W. It stands out from the 1982 crowd as one of the best designs of the year. Broadway would continue to be a revival model, also seen in *Flicky* (Sega, 1984), *Mirax* (Current Technology Inc., 1985), and other games.

ABCDEFGHIJKLM
NOPQRSTUVWXYZ
abcdefghijklm
nopqrstuvwxyz
0123456789

XEVIOUS NAMCO/1982

An innovative sci-fi shoot 'em up with a creative typeface design. The otherworldly weight distribution in G, R, b and 6 is immediately noticeable. The lowercase letters are narrower and more square than

the capitals. The fact that the designer probably did not have a background in Latin type design worked in their favour. Despite its very strong characteristics, the font was copied many times.

DINGO ASHBY COMPUTERS AND GRAPHICS LTD/1983

Ashby's only arcade game casts its player as a bear, roaming a map and eating fruit. The developer is known today as Rare. The typeface has strong stroke contrast, but is slightly inconsistent: H, I, L, T and U look rather out of place. Its aesthetics would have made the typeface a perfect fit for *Pac-Man* (see page 24).

MARBLE MADNESS ATARI GAMES/1984

The typeface above is one of two unused typefaces from *Marble Madness* (see also page 86). There is modest use of mid-tone colour in this ultra-heavy sans, and the horizontal stroke execution is so strict that some letters have high waists (A, F, P).

PAPERBOY ATARI GAMES/1984

Games often allow their players to perform outlandish tasks and quests that would be impossible to carry out in reality. However, *Paperboy* does the opposite by taking the simple task of riding a bicycle around a neighbourhood and making it extremely difficult. The typeface is a nice monolinear sans serif that does not compromise on horizontal stroke thickness. It uses the full height of the 8-pixel grid, so you cannot typeset multiple lines unless you insert another full line. The typeface was used in two other games.

FOOD FIGHT ATARI/1982

Arcade graphics eventually became powerful enough to spare resources for the development of minor elements such as type, and one of the earliest uses of a multicolour typeface was in March 1982 in *Food Fight*. This three-colour font uses two darker tones for anti-aliasing around the chunky sans serif, and looks great on the intended black background. Eleven colour palettes flash constantly on the screen, embracing this newfound graphical potential in type design.

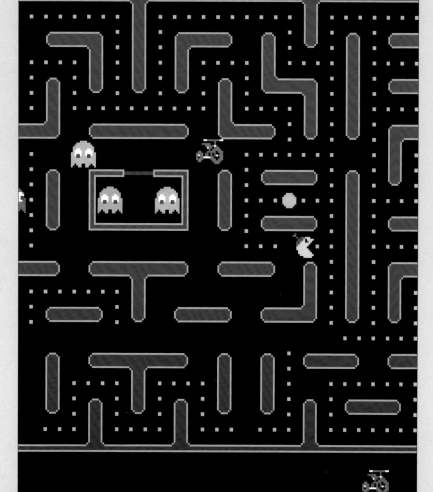

JR. PAC-MAN BALLY MIDWAY/1983

Some *Pac-Man* (see page 24) sequels, such as *Ms. Pac-Man* and *Jr. Pac-Man*, were made by the American distributor Bally Midway, without Namco's consent. Fittingly, the typeface for Jr. is entirely lowercase, but still yellow, chunky and circular, just like Pac-Man himself. The jump in brightness between the mid-tone yellows is rather large, but works fine for anti-aliasing.

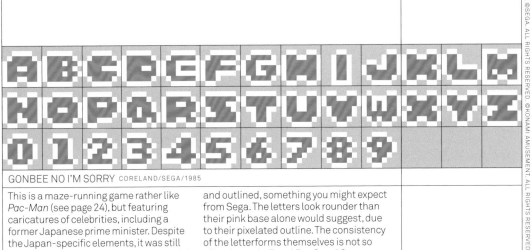

KAMIKAZE CABBIE DATA EAST/1984

In the 60s, when cars became common in Japan, cab drivers began to drive at reckless speeds in order to secure more customers and keep their business competitive. They became known as 'kamikaze taxis' and would go on to

inspire *Kamikaze Cabbie* and other games like *Crazy Taxi* (Sega, 1999). This typeface is a fairly consistent bold face, with some interesting elements like the closed G and the very tight space inside M.

GONBEE NO I'M SORRY CORELAND/SEGA/1985

This is a maze-running game rather like *Pac-Man* (see page 24), but featuring caricatures of celebrities, including a former Japanese prime minister. Despite the Japan-specific elements, it was still exported to the US. The typeface is playful

and outlined, something you might expect from Sega. The letters look rounder than their pink base alone would suggest, due to their pixelated outline. The consistency of the letterforms themselves is not so effective, as in E and F or O and Q.

TWINBEE KONAMI/1985

Twinbee is a quirky game, featuring fighter jets with boxing gloves that battle evil vegetables. It was one of the pioneers of two-player gaming. The typeface

is a high-contrast sans, with an inline decoration that makes the typeface look lighter than it is. The blue in O and 0 is aligned to opposite sides for distinction.

RAIDERS5 UPL/1985

A maze game that is more puzzle than action. The typeface first appeared the previous year in *Ninjakun Majou no Bouken* (UPL, 1984) with shadow, but not gradation or lowercase. There are similarities to Xevious (see page 48), but the stroke modulation is much more calligraphic, and the lowercase is a lot more in harmony with the uppercase. The 'middle finger Q' is not an uncommon occurance in videogame typography.

ARGUS NMK/JALECO/1986

A vertical shooter like *Valtric* (see page 58), *Argus* used a very similar typeface. The two games' exact release dates are not documented, but *Argus* was probably the later release, judging by the differences in the typeface, most notably the presence of lowercase. The letters M, N, W and X are even bolder and more daring. N is just a square with two notches, while M and W lack the middle part entirely. The ascending g is an adorable outlier.

GRIDIRON FIGHT TEHKAN/1985

Tehkan was the former name of Tecmo, and *Gridiron Fight* was an American football game. The typeface seems to have borrowed many ideas from Xevious (see page 48). The thin strokes are two pixels thick, which makes the contrast less jarring and letters more legible, and the lowercase f is reversed.

02 SANS BOLD

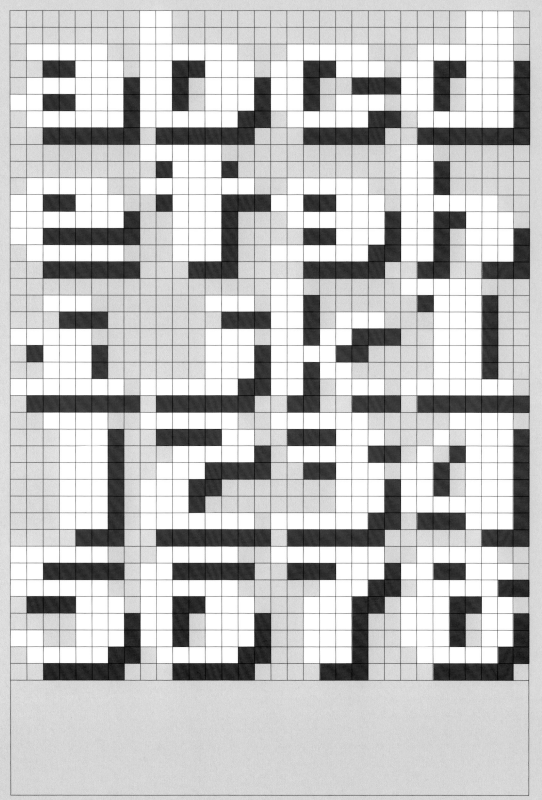

FANTASY ZONE SEGA/1986

A quintessential cute 'em up, rubbing shoulders with *Twinbee* (see page 52) and *Parodius* (see pages 66, 87 and 89). Sega continues its love affair with outlined typefaces here, but reduces the letter size and adds ample spacing.

The design may not look particularly noteworthy, but in comparison with Taito's similar *Rastan Saga* type (see page 181), you can see it is easy to get caught up in originality and forget to make a typeface work.

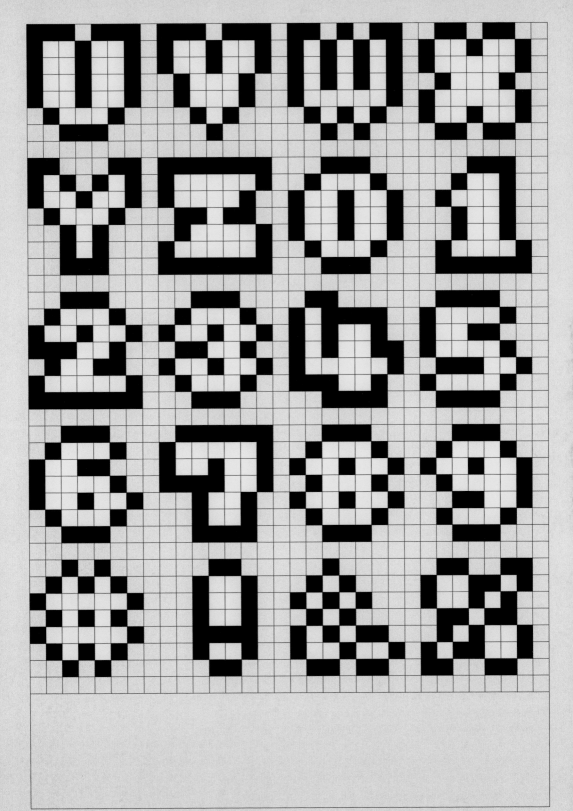

VALTRIC NMK/JALECO/1986

In this vertical shooter, the player controls a hovering vehicle that can shoot in eight directions and also jump. The typeface is prominently bold, cramming just as much as you can get into the 8×8 grid without sacrificing legibility. It is rather unassuming, but demonstrates how to make a bold typeface.

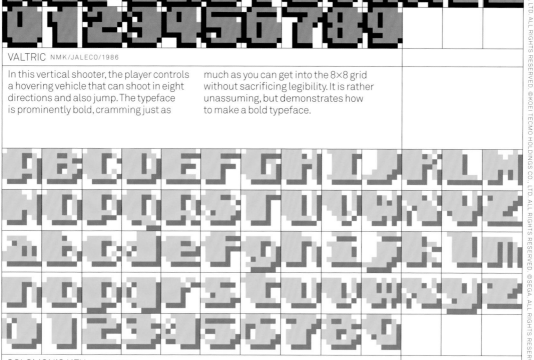

SOLOMON'S KEY TECMO/1986

A fantasy single-screen puzzle game in which the players must find keys to progress. The typeface appears to be an offshoot of Gridiron Fight (see page 54), something more evident in the numerals than the capitals. The fun part is the lowercase, which retains a Xevious-like unconventional placement of thick strokes (see page 48). The lowercase a looks ridiculous, and I absolutely love it.

ALIEN SYNDROME SEGA/1987

You are in a spaceship infested by aliens, shooting your way out. You could argue this is a light sans with two layers of extrusion, but I consider it a bold sans with highlights, as the white layers do not align (J doesn't descend as far as I). Readers may remember the game's typography for its 16×16 adaptation of Letraset's Stop, which was also used in *After Burner* (see page 62) as an 8×8 typeface.

02 SANS BOLD

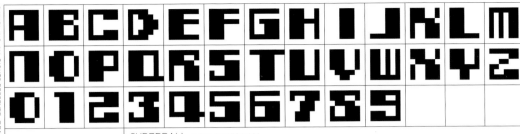

CYBERBALL ATARI GAMES/1988

Cyberball answers the often-posed question of what American football might look like if it were played by robots. This bold and oddly contrasted typeface belongs to the Xevious subcategory

(see page 48), and possibly takes inspiration from *Tecmo Bowl* (Tecmo, 1987). It is more square, and similar to early Williams fonts (see page 15).

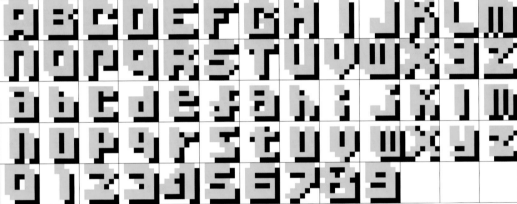

ASSAULT NAMCO/1988

A vertical shoot 'em up with a tank that can turn in any direction and also jump. The setting rotates and scales around the player, instead of the player moving around on screen. This heavy square sans retains

much of its personality with corner-cuts, in O for example, odd choices such as the semi-stencil P and 4, and lowercase-like Q. It is unclear as to whether the 8 was a deliberate design choice.

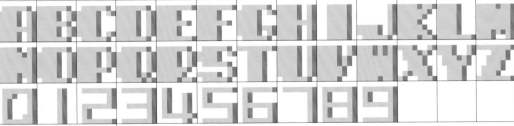

R–TYPE II IREM/1989

R-Type's font was a loose imitation of *Gradius* (see page 86), but instead of refining the design, Irem wisely chose to seek its own visual identity for the sequel. Two competing franchises, *Gradius* and *Darius* (see page 78), were

using light and regular sans respectively, so bold seemed like a logical choice. The strict application of thickness to the left sides results in a couple of odd characters. Both J and S are wrong in the calligraphic sense.

ARGUS
NMK/JALECO/1986

SOLOMON'S KEY
TECMO/1986

AFTER BURNER SEGA/1987

A flight action game strongly inspired by the film *Top Gun* (Paramount Pictures, 1986). While the logo is based on Brignall's Revue type from Letraset, the game's main typeface is inspired by Stop, a font designed by Aldo Novarese in 1970. However, the *After Burner* face is thicker and takes some liberties. H, K and R are complete forms, and X is no longer comprised of half circles, for example. These changes are sensible, considering that Stop is a highly illegible typeface designed to be displayed at large sizes.

SCORE
6708

LINES
9

LEVEL
3

NEXT

ABCDEFGHIJKLM
NOPQRSTUVWXYZ
0123456789

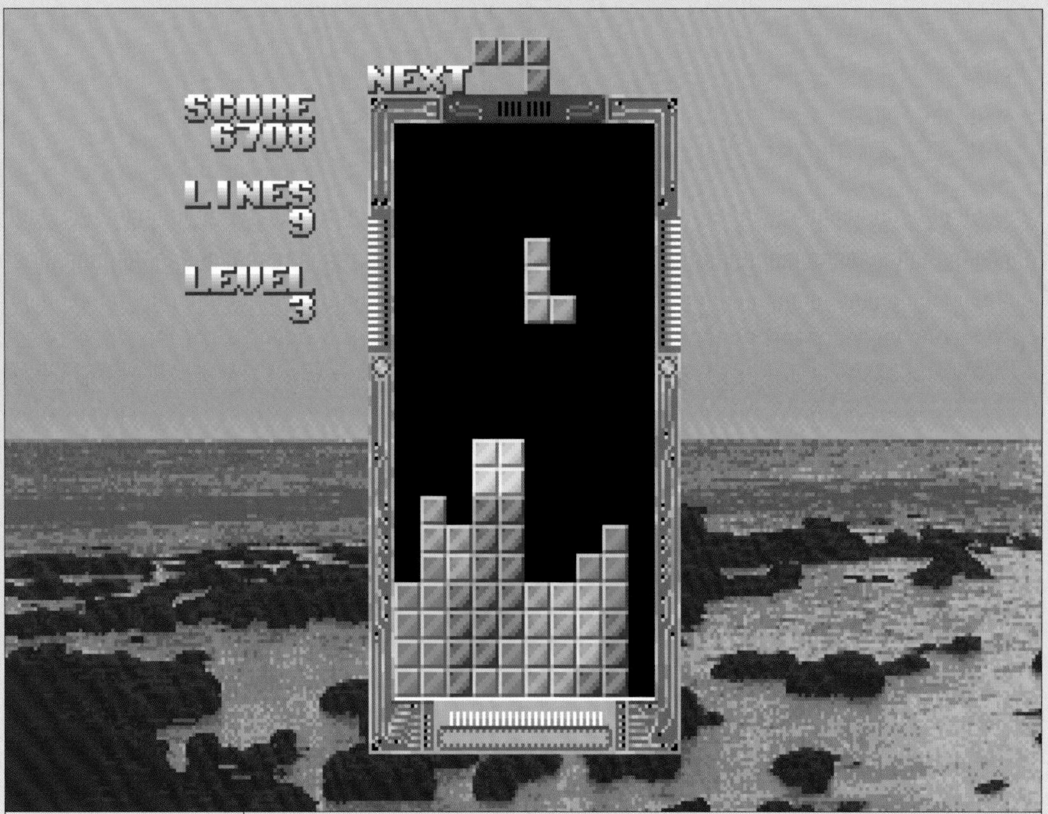

TETRIS SEGA/1988

There were two arcade releases of *Tetris* in 1988, one by Atari and another by Sega. The Sega version has beautiful backgrounds, a chimpanzee teaching players how to play the game and, of course, this nicely coloured bold sans.

The diagonals seem either too thick or not thick enough. Atari's *Tetris* typeface, on the other hand, is simply Quiz Show (see pages 18 and 44–45) with a flipped R to hint at its Russian origin.

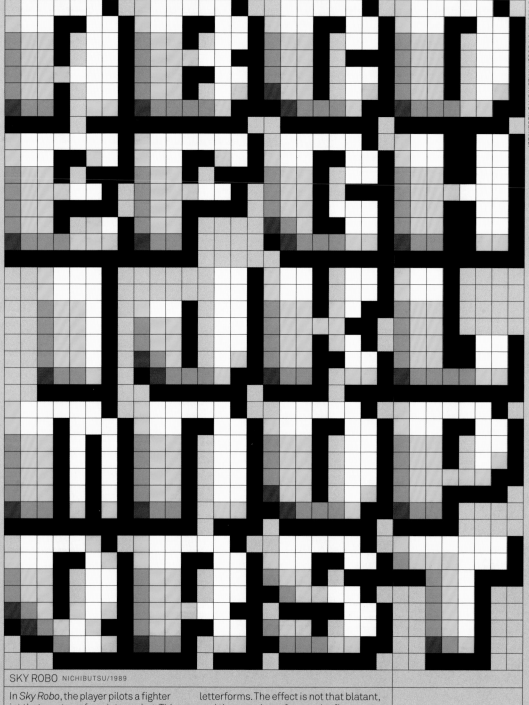

SKY ROBO NICHIBUTSU/1989

In *Sky Robo*, the player pilots a fighter jet that can transform into a robot. This typeface looks as though the Adobe Photoshop emboss effect was applied to the square before it was carved into letterforms. The effect is not that blatant, and there are lots of manual refinements. Varying stem widths are not as jarring as they are in other typefaces, since the embossing obscures the issue.

02 SANS BOLD

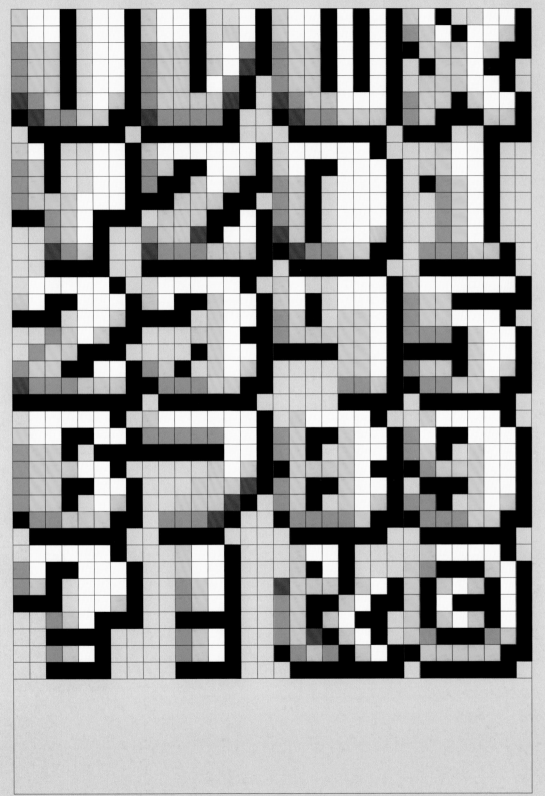

CREDIT 0

― 神話からお笑いへ ―

PLEASE DEPOSIT COIN

1ST BONUS AT 20000 PTS
2ND BONUS AT 80000 PTS

© KONAMI 1990

PARODIUS DA! KONAMI/1990

This cute 'em up takes a drastically different artistic direction from *Gradius* (see page 86). This adorable typeface is spot on for the comic tone of the game and has a similar look to Gill Sans ExtraBold (aka Gill Kayo), which is a popular choice for comedy film posters. The placement of counter shapes is playful, and especially successful in the numerals, whereas in the capitals the horizontal strokes could be more unified. The N, for example, seems to be a pixel too thick at the top.

COTTON SUCCESS/SEGA/1991

A young witch girl, who loves eating, is persuaded to save the world in return for candy. This cute, rounded, bold face was used in a number of sequels and became the standard *Cotton* typeface. It makes a distinction between similarly structured letters by using contrast differently: see B/8, O/0, and S/5.

SNOW BROS. TOAPLAN/1990

A single-screen co-op game in which players control snowmen who make and roll snowballs. The graphics are comical and colourful, and the typeface complements them well. The simple three-colour gradation looks great in all four available palettes. The vertical thickness is three pixels on the left, and two on the right, which creates a unique M and W.

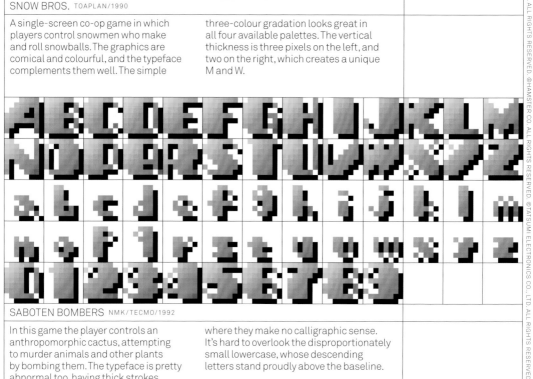

SABOTEN BOMBERS NMK/TECMO/1992

In this game the player controls an anthropomorphic cactus, attempting to murder animals and other plants by bombing them. The typeface is pretty abnormal too, having thick strokes where they make no calligraphic sense. It's hard to overlook the disproportionately small lowercase, whose descending letters stand proudly above the baseline.

BIG FIGHT: BIG TROUBLE IN THE ATLANTIC OCEAN TATSUMI/1992

The aim of the game is to stop a battleship, disguised as a cruise ship by an evil organization, by punching everyone on board. This beat 'em up can also be a versus game if you have a second player.

The very large lowercase, especially the single-storey a, is the best part. The notch of the r is misaligned with the stem, which is clever and a common technique.

02 SANS BOLD

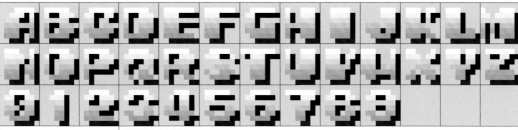

TERRA DIVER RAIZING/EIGHTING/1996

A shoot 'em up with a narrative and strong Japanese typographic style influenced by *Neon Genesis Evangelion* (Bandai, 1999). It is easy to overlook the small Latin face used in the game, which is not in the same tone but is unique in its own right. The uppercase, especially Q, is the most fun aspect, being less calligraphic than the numerals and lowercase.

DANCE DANCE REVOLUTION 4TH MIX KONAMI/2000

This font was possibly based on Antique Olive (Roger Excoffon, *c.* 1960), using its thickest weight. The faultless lowercase height alignment is made possible by giving descenders enough room, making character heights a pixel shorter than other typical designs. Sometimes, using fewer pixels actually improves the design. It also has a gradient emboss for good measure; a subtle yet masterful detail.

MATRIMELEE NOISE FACTORY/ATLUS/2003

A sequel to the fighting game *Power Instinct* (see page 115). It uses several typefaces, but this high-score font draws the most attention. Compared to previous entries, it is a huge step up, a confident design from the final years of pixel fonts. Unfortunately, the in-game use mostly consists of numerals, which explains why the issue of G being identical to 0 was not addressed.

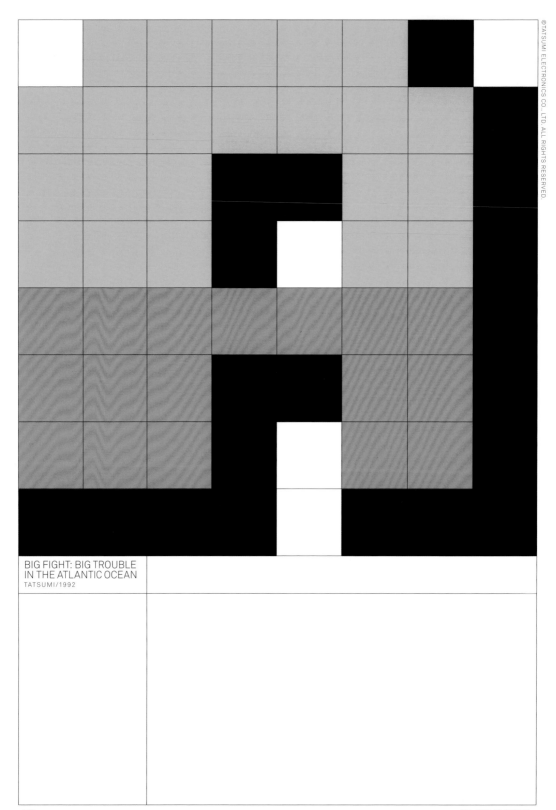

BIG FIGHT: BIG TROUBLE
IN THE ATLANTIC OCEAN
TATSUMI/1992

02 SANS BOLD

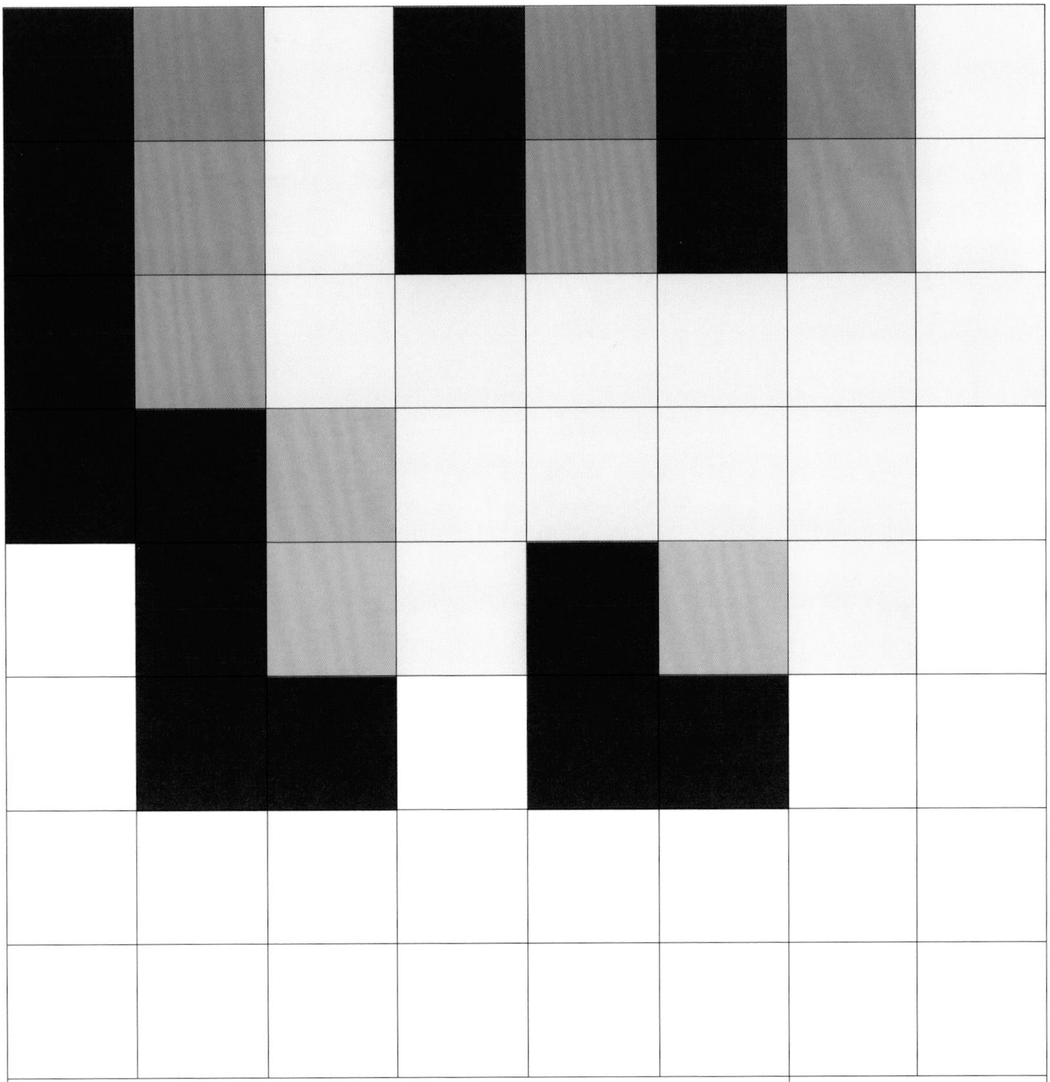

DANCE DANCE
REVOLUTION 4TH MIX
KONAMI/2000

FIRE BARREL IREM/1993

A vertical shoot 'em up that was not particularly successful, but one that's recommended for newcomers to the genre thanks to its low level of difficulty. The typeface is packed with graphical effects, featuring gradation, shadow and emboss effect, then extra gradation on the edges. The 1 is rarely picked as the best character in a typeface, but here it deserves that accolade.

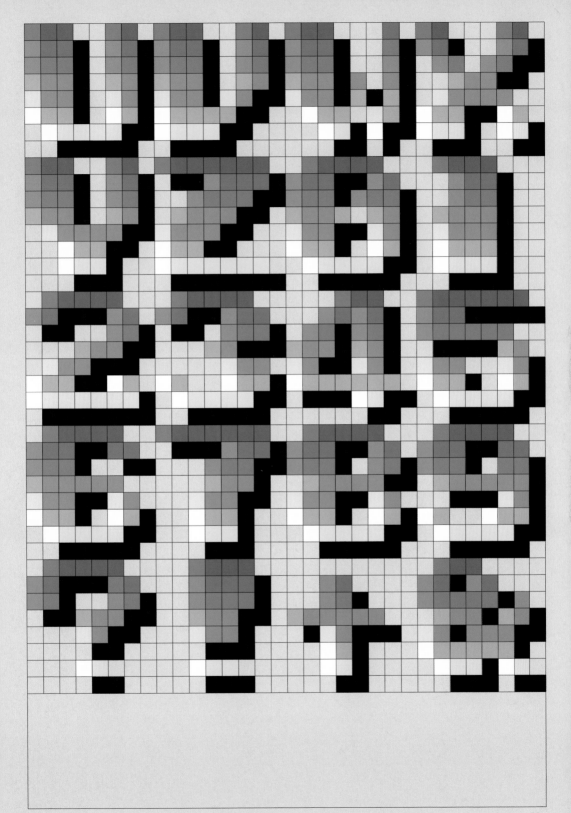

ANATOMY OF THE ATARI FONT

Is it possible to make a high-resolution version of a low-resolution typeface? Can Quiz Show be made into a modern, vectorized font that captures all the designer's intentions, but without the pixelated feel? How do you make sense of each pixel, and what is happening with that Q?

1. Atari Quiz Show typeface.
2. Hard interpretation.
3. Soft interpretation.
4. Harmonized interpretation.

When you make an 8×8-pixel typeface, you need to have realistic creative goals. You may have wanted a nice slope to the sides of your A, but you may need to break the shape into an octagon or square to give enough space for the counter. You may want to have a 1-pixel-wide notch inside your Y, but it is impossible to keep the letter's symmetry if the stem thickness is an even number. A future designer who wants to unpack such details will have no choice but to guess at the original intentions behind the pixels.

Let's take Quiz Show as our example (see pages 18 and 44–45). The ambitious design of some pixel shapes is difficult to implement across the entire set of characters: the bowls of C, D and G don't match A's artistic slope. C, D and G share the same delicate curvature, but B, J, O, P, Q, R, S and U are less rounded on the outside, and their inside corners are completely square. It also seems strange to apply different roundnesses to C and O.

Moving past these major inconsistencies to focus on the details, R has a strong corner on the middle right. Should this be a corner? If you were the font's designer deciding about the placement of this extra pixel, you might think its existence would not make a smooth transition, but its absence could make the stroke thickness weak and the top bowl would become very pointy. Common sense would suggest that the corner was intended to be round. The Q's tail is very hard and the O's shape is disrupted in order to keep the tail sticking out

by cutting in. These designs only make sense in a pixel format, but what do you do with that?

The calligraphic model of S should have the thick part in the middle, not on the sides. Each stroke of X ends thickly, unlike K or R, which have the calligraphic stroke contrast. You might want to just apply the same logic to all three letters, but the presence of the extra pixels around X cannot be so easily ignored. After all, one might say it's a memorable detail that makes this typeface unique. The numbers appear largely straightforward, apart from 0.

The visual language of low-resolution design relies on ambiguity, which sounds contrary to what is squarely visible on-screen. Each pixel has a story behind it. Unpacking this story is a technical and aesthetic challenge and harder than scaling down. At such a low level of resolution, no computer can correctly rebuild the original beauty of the typeface – at least not better than we can.

Different designs

There is no denying that a high-resolution version of this typeface would be a moderately contrasted sans serif, but if you give the same upscaling task to five different designers, you will end up with five different answers.

Opposite and on the next two pages are three different approaches: universally diagonal, universally round and a more liberally harmonized solution. The first does not stray far

from the original and thus fails to become a high-resolution update. The second is perhaps more natural, but strays too far and emphasizes the internal inconsistencies too much. The harmonized font offers a good middle ground, although it still clearly shows the low-resolution origins of the typeface.

Examples of attempts to scale up Quiz Show can be found in the arcade from as early as 1977. *Super Bug* (Atari, 1977) has a 16×16-pixel version of the typeface that is riddled with errors. There is an unexpected calligraphic touch that makes asymmetric bowl shapes in letters such as C. The spine of S is thin, but more diagonal. U is not quite symmetric, X is strangely pixelated on the left, Y is thicker on the left, 3 now has a beak, and there seems to be a misplaced pixel in 8. The design was then updated and completed in the same year in *Drag Race* (see page 78), where the R's bowl becomes symmetric, Q is fairly faithful to the original, S has a thicker spine, U is unprofessional and Z also has a beak. The number 8 loses its calligraphic spine and becomes symmetric.

Taito released *Darius* (see page 78) in 1986 – a horizontal spaceship shooter known for its gigantic cabinet, with three CRT displays chained horizontally, offering a very wide field of view. The base typeface therefore had to be large, and a 16×16-pixel version of the *Pac-Man* font (see page 24) was used. The result is more consistent. C is interpreted

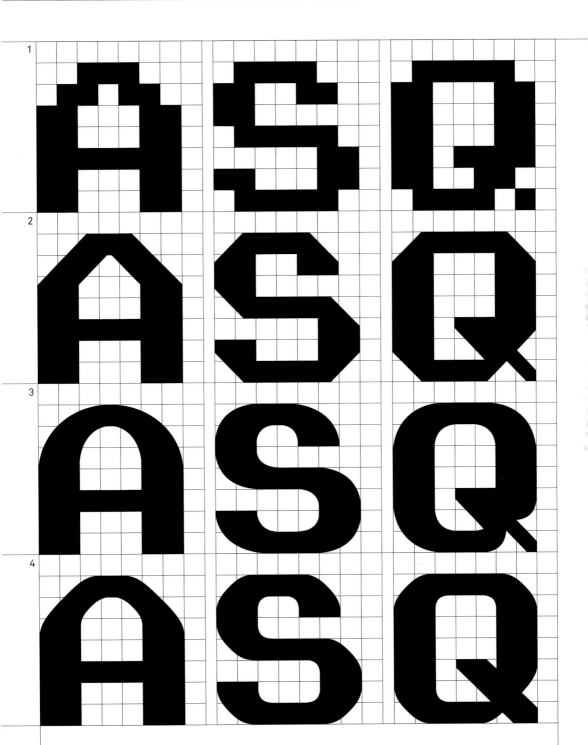

5. Atari Quiz Show typeface.

6. Hard interpretation.

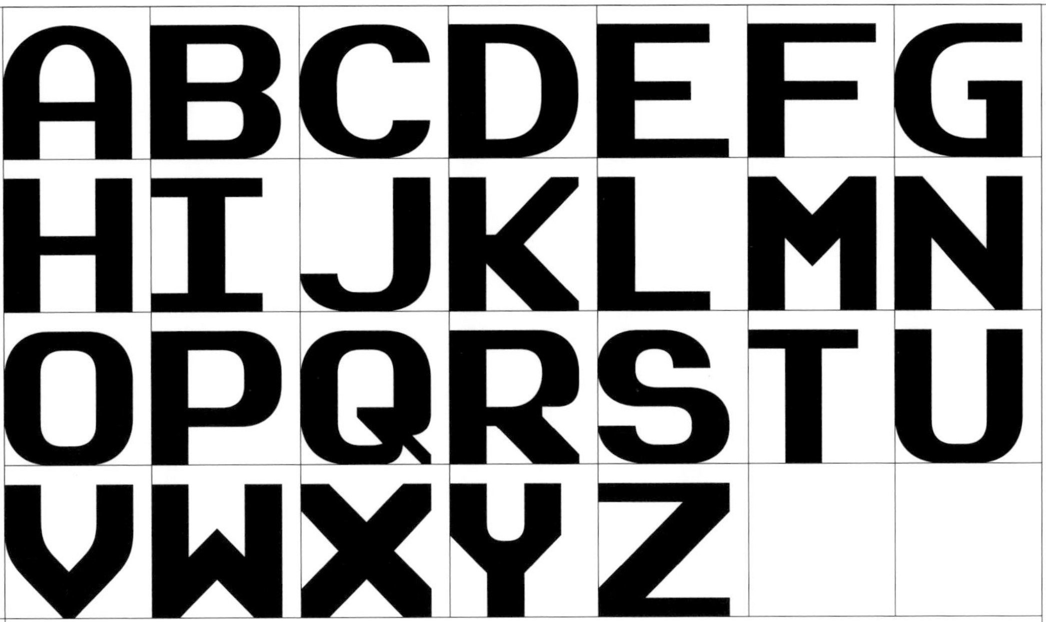

ABCDEFG
HIJKLMN
OPQRSTU
VWXYZ

7. Soft interpretation.

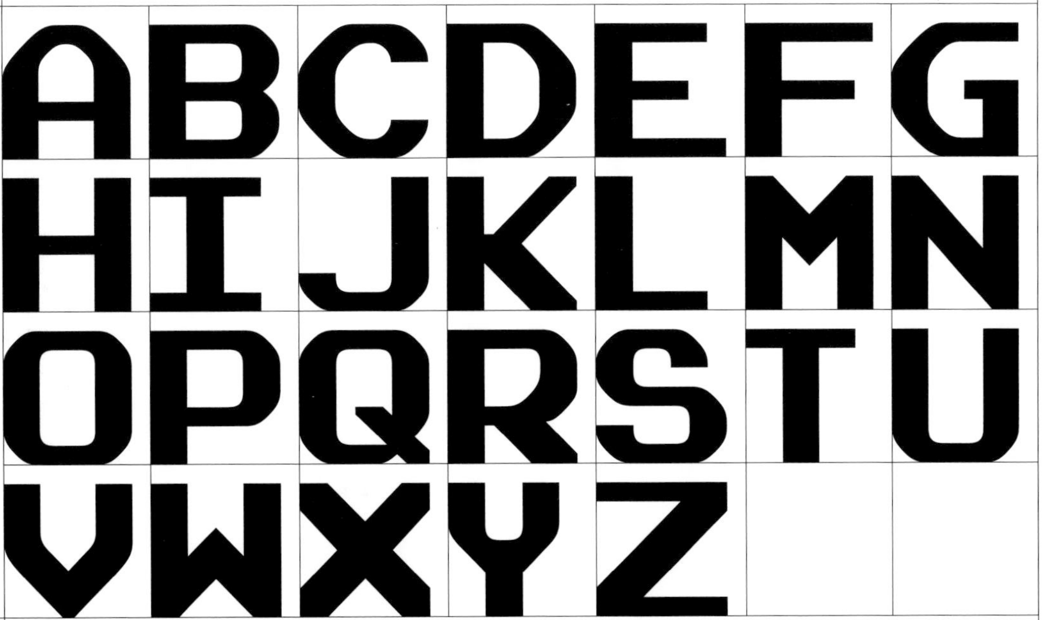

ABCDEFG
HIJKLMN
OPQRSTU
VWXYZ

8. Harmonized interpretation.

ANATOMY OF THE ATARI FONT

10. Drag Race, Atari, 1977.

11. Darius, Taito, 1986.

as diagonal, unlike J or S, despite having the same shape as the original 8×8. Namco's *Driver's Eyes*'s font from 1990 is closer to Atari's (see below). It has some stroke thickness inconsistency in P, the S has no contrast and the round shapes and 45° diagonals in A, V and Y do not quite work. Namco released *Tank Force* the next year, with more Darius-like angular flavour. All of the previous games mentioned have a pointed notch inside Y, but this Y is square.

Upscaling attempts such as these are not straightforward and seldom successful. Outside the gaming world, type designer Charles Bigelow made a vector version of Apple's Chicago typeface, originally created by Suzan Kare as a pack of bitmap fonts.* While Bigelow's effort is gallant, it again shows the problem of converting a font to function in an environment in which the quirks of low-resolution design are no longer forgiven.

* Inside the Chicago font file were multiple sets of bitmaps pixelated for different sizes. Square – a Japanese company known for quality role-playing games – seemed to like the design. The same Chicago design is used in *Final Fantasy VI* (1994) and *Chrono Trigger* (1995).

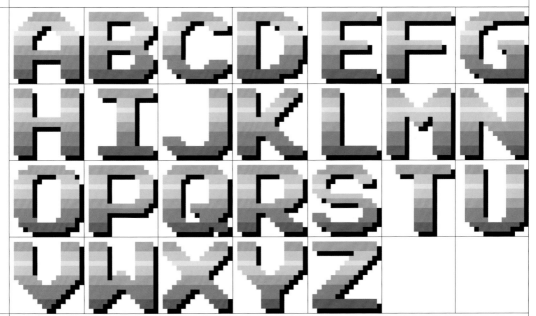

12. Driver's Eyes, Namco, 1991.

03

SANS LIGHT

COPS 'N ROBBERS ATARI/1976

Although not as long-lived as the *Quiz Show* typeface (see pages 18 and 44–45), *Cops 'N Robbers* also features a well-executed design. There are some letters that could be improved, notably R and 4, but the basic design was good enough to ensure that the typeface, with modifications, was used widely across the industry.

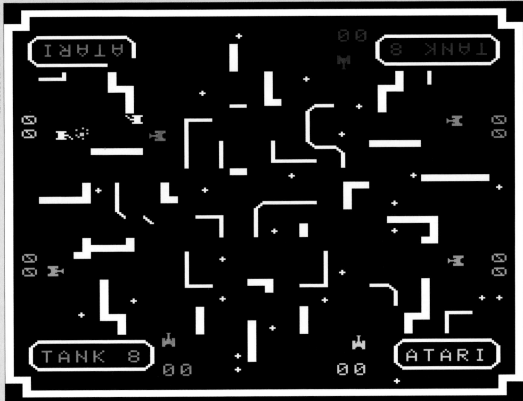

A B C D E F G H I J K L M
N O P Q R S T U V W X Y Z
0 1 2 3 4 5 6 7 8 9

TANK 8 ATARI/1976

Tank 8 and *Cops 'N Robbers* (see opposite) were both released in 1976. A close inspection of the two typefaces indicates that *Tank 8* came out later, as its font has a better design: C is symmetric, R is better harmonized with other letters, 4 is not as short, and the numerals are centred. This version became popular, used notably by Taito in *Space Invaders* (see page 84).

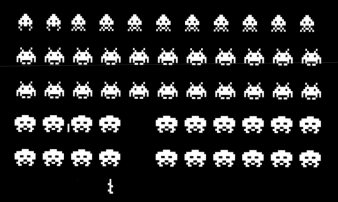

SPACE INVADERS TAITO/1978

Taito sold jukeboxes and distributed Atari games in Japan, making table-shaped arcade cabinets to be used in cafés. The most successful of these was *Space Invaders*. Although I was not alive to experience the craze first-hand, I played hundreds of clone games during my research and thus became painfully aware of its popularity. The original game, and most of the clones, featured the above typeface, copied from *Tank 8* (see page 83) with a minor modification to M.

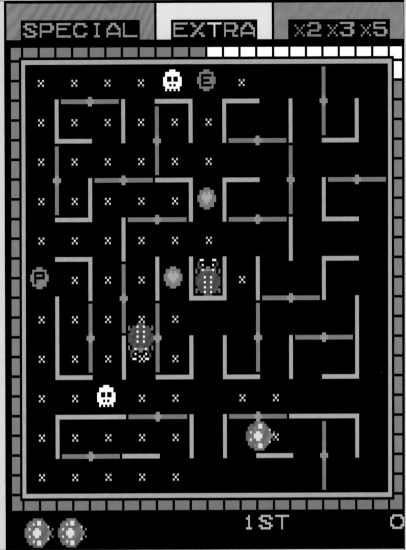

SPECIAL EXTRA x2 x3 x5

1ST 0

ABCDEFGHIJKLM
NOPQRSTUVWXYZ
0123456789

LADY BUG UNIVERSAL/1981

An insect-themed maze-runner similar to *Pac-Man* (see page 24). The typeface is light and round, and six pixels high. Sometimes, if diagonal pixels only touch at the corners, they can look thinner than the horizontals and verticals, creating disparity in the typeface. Here the diagonal pixels touch at the sides, avoiding inconsistency and making the strokes look thicker. The designer has then used the disjointed effect of corner connection advantageously in K, Q and X.

MARBLE MADNESS ATARI GAMES/1984

This thin Art Deco sans was the second unused typeface in *Marble Madness* (see also page 49), later used in *Road Blasters* (Atari, 1987). The second colour is used effectively, to make the stroke appear one and a half pixels thick rather than to achieve a shadow effect. The credited

designer and graphics programmer is Mark Cerny, who was only eighteen at the time. Cerny later worked as a programmer for *Sonic the Hedgehog 2* (Sega, 1992), and eventually became lead architect and producer of the PlayStation 4 and PlayStation Vita.

GRADIUS KONAMI/1985

There is a good chance that anyone who played *Gradius* would be able to name the game after seeing the isolated typeface. It is a unique design from an iconic game, consisting mostly of vertical, horizontal, and 45° diagonal lines. Its rigid squareness may remind keen

typographers of Wim Crouwel's 1967 typeface New Alphabet. The shadow angle is one pixel to the right and down in principle, but that is ignored in some cases. Konami's puzzle game *Cue Brick* (1989) used this typeface and added a lowercase.

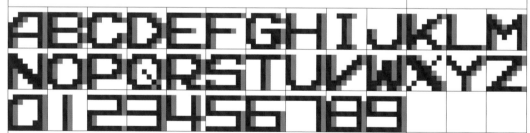

R-TYPE IREM/1987

Irem's take on the horizontal shoot 'em up in *R-Type*, along with *Gradius* (above) and *Darius* (see page 78), saw the heyday of the genre in the 80s. The game also marked the return of Irem, which had been suffering financially at the time.

The rounds and verticals of the type are partially rounded, or otherwise strictly 45° diagonal, and letter thickness is loosely controlled. In later uses, the thinness of the typeface was abandoned in favour of a bold style.

03 SANS LIGHT

SPY HUNTER 2 BALLY MIDWAY/1987

Unlike the first game's font, which was an ill-executed roman (see page 108), this is a square sans with a technical aesthetic. Every letter apart from I fills the square almost completely, which makes letter spacing tight and consistent. The diagonal strokes in B, D, M and W are drawn solid instead of touching at the corners.

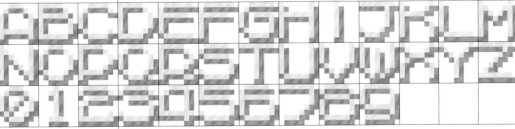

DIAMOND RUN KH VIDEO/1989

A cave-mining game similar to *Boulder Dash* (First Star Software, 1984) where the player must tunnel underground to release buried rocks, causing them to fall onto gemstones and enemies in order to gain points. The game was developed and published by Kyle Hodgetts, so this round typeface is most likely his creation. The looping Z and 2 immediately grab one's attention, followed by the symmetrical 6 and 9. The typeface is the game's most attractive graphical asset.

PARODIUS DA! KONAMI/1990

The typeface above was created as a second font for *Parodius Da!* but never used. In the end, Konami decided to use an ultra-bold style in the game (see page 66). The basic structure of this much thinner typeface is completely different to that of the primary font, but it conveys a similar degree of fun with rounded corners and exaggerated counter-shape sizes.

MARBLE MADNESS
ATARI GAMES/1984

PARODIUS DA!
KONAMI/1990

GRADIUS III KONAMI/1989

Konami improved its typeface for this second sequel, featuring a more rounded but still very mechanical look. The B, D, P and R have the top left open, and the shadows no longer leave a gap between the main stroke, as in V, X and 7. The spacing of J could be improved by moving the letter to the left.

CREDIT 01   HI   80000   TIME 3:17
1UP   1500

POWER

2

BIG KARNAK GAELCO/1991

In *Big Karnak*, the player is an armed
pharaoh, killing mummies, zombies,
and all sorts of Egyptian baddies.
This typeface plays a secondary role
to a thicker and more colourful version.

The base letterform falls under the Tank 8
category (see page 83), and the lowercase
sometimes uses capital forms, which is
unconventional.

ROBOCOP 2 DATA EAST/1991

A well-received beat 'em up sequel to *RoboCop* (1988). Data East did not have to look far for typographic inspiration, as the movie featured an iconic display interface with blocky green type, which the designers had already adapted for the first game. The numerals are the tallest and lowercase shortest, but the ascender height varies, as b, d and h are shorter than f, i, j, k, l and t.

CAPTAIN AMERICA AND THE AVENGERS DATA EAST/1991

Originally made for *Captain America*'s side-scrolling brawler, the game developer made use of this typeface on several occasions, including for *Tumblepop* (Data East, 1991). Its uppercase is a mature design with a well-crammed W. The x looks out of place, perhaps influenced by the designer's education in mathematics. The g is cute, and the bowls' proportion is similar to that of ITC Souvenir.

03 SANS LIGHT

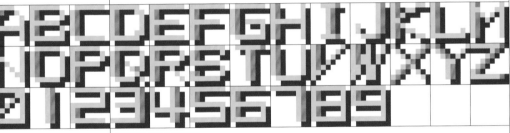

SPIDER-MAN: THE VIDEOGAME SEGA/1991

Franchise beat 'em ups were mostly the domain of Konami in the early 90s, but Sega also had a good piece of the action. This outlined sans serif with a hint of Art Deco styling is not really a signature of the comic, but feels natural in the game. Apart from the spacing problem, similar to that in *X-Men* (below) but in the lowercase, it is a confident and stylish typeface. The height and baseline of the lowercase are well executed too.

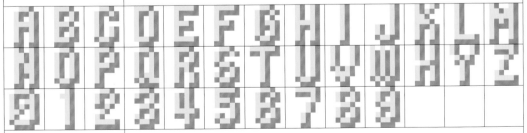

XEXEX KONAMI/1991

It's easy to guess from the font that this game was developed by the same team that made *Gradius* (see page 86) – the numbers are similar, and the designer missed the mark with the W in the same way. The beautiful two-layer shadow is applied only where there is enough space. The game is a horizontal shooter and visually ambitious, making use of transparency, rotation, scaling and warping.

X-MEN KONAMI/1992

There are many excellent wide typeface designs in 8×8 format, but condensed ones are scarce and Konami's *X-Men* typeface demonstrates why. It is a well-designed typeface, with no problems in the letterforms. The issue with condensed type is that you cannot tighten the spacing between characters. So, when typed out, the letters are sprinkled sparsely and do not hold together well to form a word.

THUNDER DRAGON NMK/TECMO/1991

In the vertical shooter game *Thunder Dragon*, the design of the jet is heavily influenced by the UD-4L Cheyenne Dropship in *Aliens* (20th Century Fox, 1986). The typeface is a high-waist sans with a gradation from cold grey to orange to create a heated-steel effect. The numerals are too wide at the bottom in places.

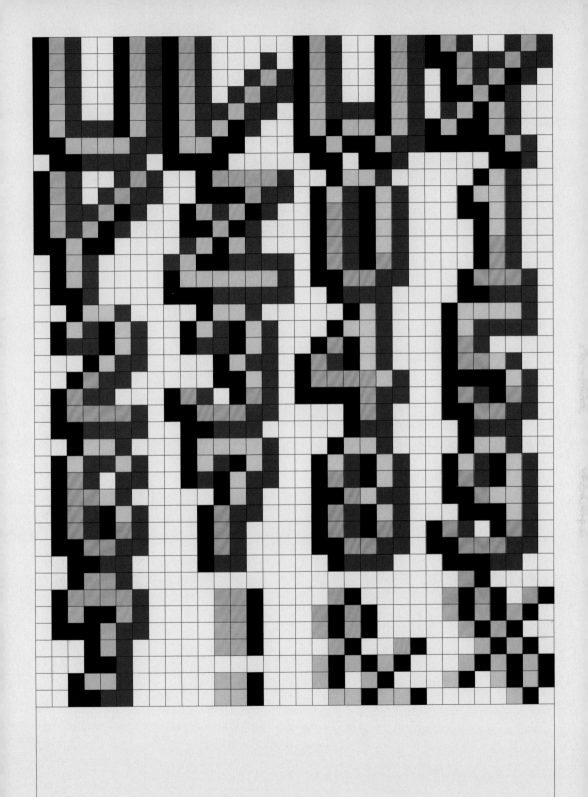

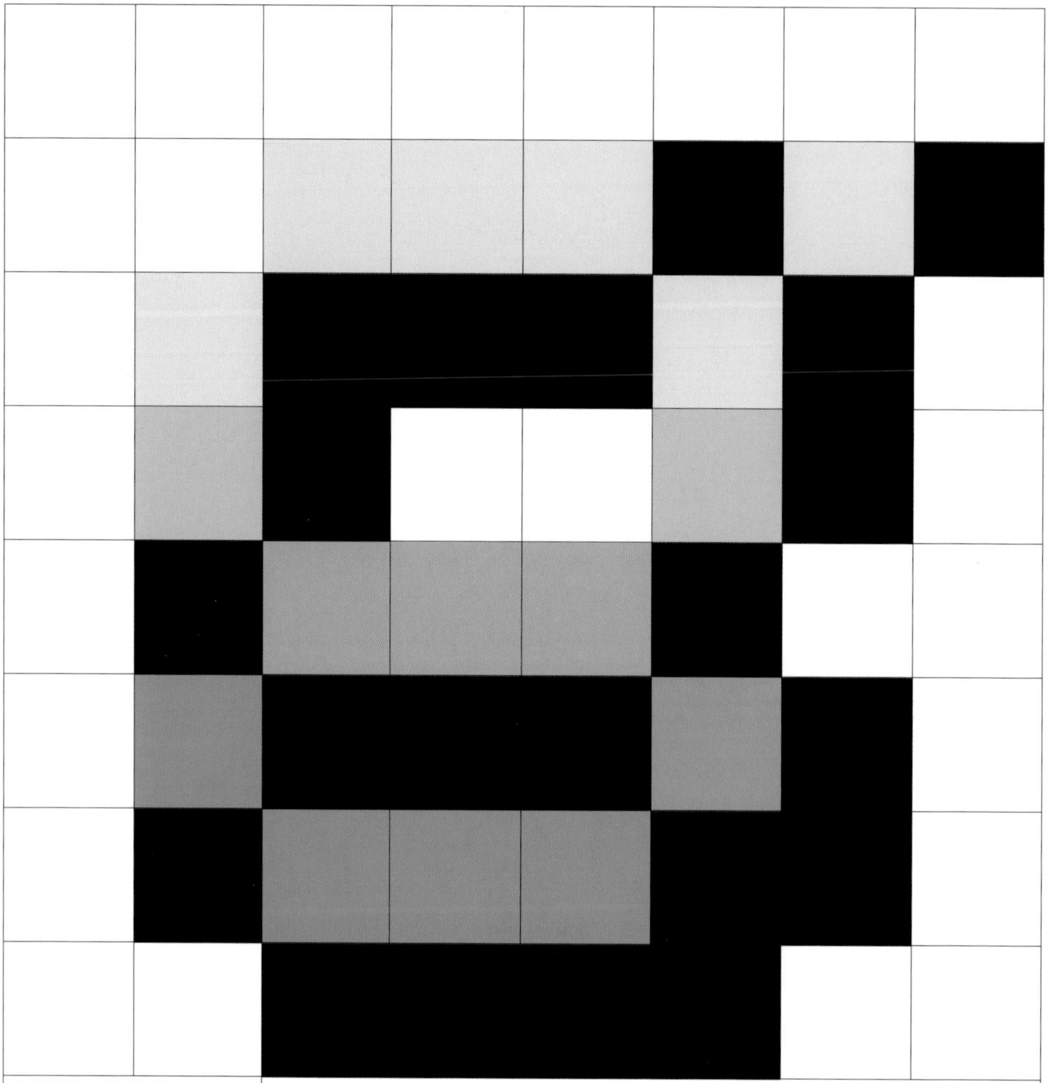

CAPTAIN AMERICA AND
THE AVENGERS
DATA EAST/1991

T-MEK
ATARI GAMES/1994

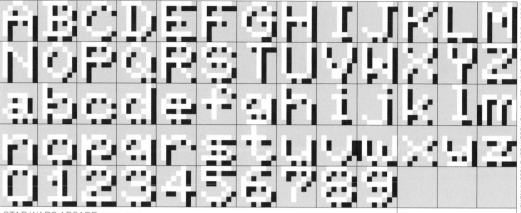

STAR WARS ARCADE SEGA/1993

Sega's 3D space shooter was later ported to 32X. There were two typefaces, and this, the first, became commonplace in Model 1 console games. The 2-pixel valley of M and square top-right corner of the lowercase a are the signature details. The fractured shadow layer is not an error, but exactly how it appears in the game.

GALS PANIC II: SPECIAL EDITION KANEKO/1994

This thin, technically stencil, typeface is similar to *Gradius III*'s (see page 90), but more rounded. The *Gals Panic* releases are eroge (erotic) games, so perhaps its inspiration was neon tube lettering. The design is not very consistent, and the A's crossbar is just a pixel, which is a risk in terms of legibility.

OUTFOXIES NAMCO/1994

A fighting game pitting seven contract killers against one another. The game boasts seven 8×8 typefaces, which is the largest number used in a single arcade game. The typeface above is the smallest of them, using a minimal amount of capital height, generous horizontal proportions, and an outline, making it well spaced. The serifs on the D are a nice touch too. The placement of every pixel has to be carefully considered when creating such small type – there is far less room for error.

ABCDEFGHIJKLM
NOPQRSTUVWXYZ
abcdefghijklm
nopqrstuvwxyz
0123456789

T-MEK ATARI GAMES/1994

Since this is a tank-based shooter, and most of the shootouts take place on the ground, the wide proportion of the typeface might have been influenced by the horizontal nature of the gameplay.

The height of the lowercase matches the uppercase, but is positioned a pixel higher in the grid and is, overall, more square. The lowercase x has quite a bold design.

ABCDEFGHIJKLM
NOPQRSTUVWXYZ
abcdefghijklm
nopqrstuvwxyz
0123456789

SALAMANDER 2 KONAMI/1996

Salamander, also known as *Life Force*, featured both horizontal and vertical shooting. This sequel was released ten years after the original game. The series as a whole is a branch of *Gradius* (see page 86), which stars the same fighter jets, Vic Viper and Lord British. The primary typeface used in the game (see page 163)

is a rather organic slanted design. This secondary face was used for the ending credits and high-score screen. Its thin strokes and square details, though inconsistent, hint at the series it originates from. It's an unconventional but functional choice for a secondary style.

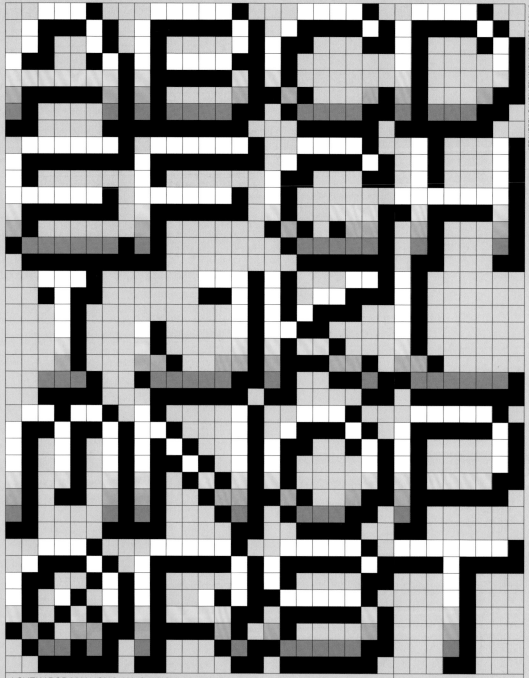

LOVELY POP MAHJONG JANGJANG SHIMASHO VISCO/1996

Erotic *Mahjong* was popular in Japanese arcades – players could see naked women after completing each level. Despite the game's mature nature, its difficulty and social aspect served as an age barrier, enabling pornographic Mahjong to coexist with youngsters' games in arcades. This is one such game with a pretty typeface. It is generally a semi-rounded thin sans with some playful letters, most notably the U.

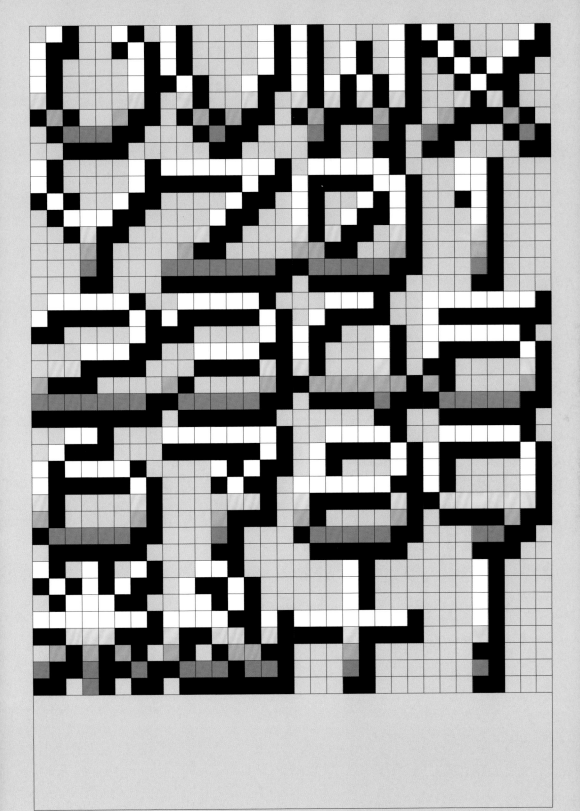

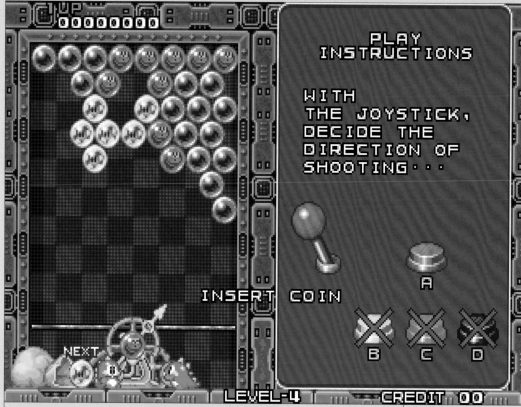

PUZZLE BOBBLE TAITO/1994

A puzzle spin-off of *Bubble Bobble* (Taito, 1986), and known in the US as *Bust-a-Move*. The popular game was cloned many times over. Its typeface was originally designed for the Japan-exclusive *Quiz Jinsei Gekijoh* (Taito, 1992). It is just a thin skeleton with outline and anti-aliasing, but its unobtrusive design has hardly any flaws.

PLANET ROZALIS

CLASS :

CYCLE OF REVOLUTION : 513
CYCLE OF ROTATION : 1.4

AMOUNT OF RADIATION :
NUMBER OF SATELLITES :
RADIUS OF EQUATOR :

VOLUME : 0.78
MASS : 0.85
DENSITY : 6.03ᵍ/ᶜᵐ
GRAVITY : 0.8

OK.

LEVEL-4   CREDIT 01

ABCDEFGHIJKLM
NOPQRSTUVWXYZ
0123456789

GALAXY FIGHT – UNIVERSAL WARRIORS SUNSOFT/1995

A 2D fighting game that takes place in space. Neo Geo-based fighting games normally had four attack buttons, but this sacrifices one for a taunting animation. The game uses Novarese's Stop typeface and American Type Founders' 1968 typeface OCR-A for big fonts, and the main 8×8 font is a Quiz Show clone (see pages 18 and 44–45). The small face above was used for the map selection screen, and is a fairly faithful adaptation of OCR-A, but with varied diagonal stroke angles.

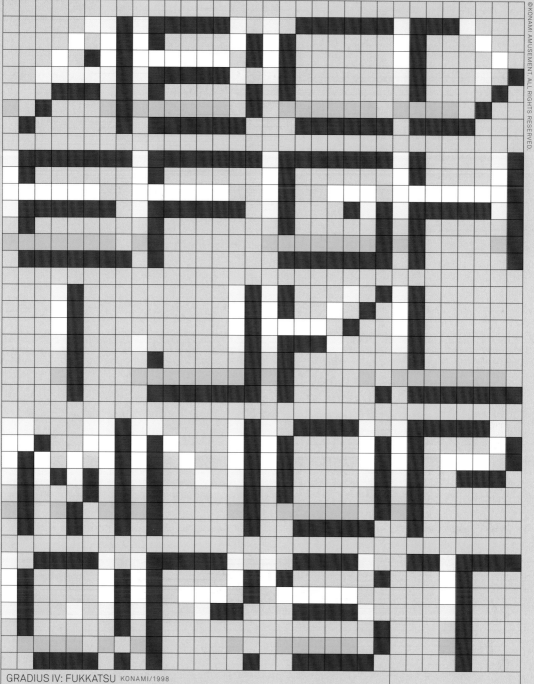

GRADIUS IV: FUKKATSU KONAMI/1998

In 1998, Konami made *Fukkatsu* (meaning 'resurrection' in Japanese). The typeface revisits the first *Gradius* (see page 86), with minor rounding as seen in *Gradius III* (see page 90). Unfortunately, G, J and the numerals are still square, which makes the face the least consistent of the three.

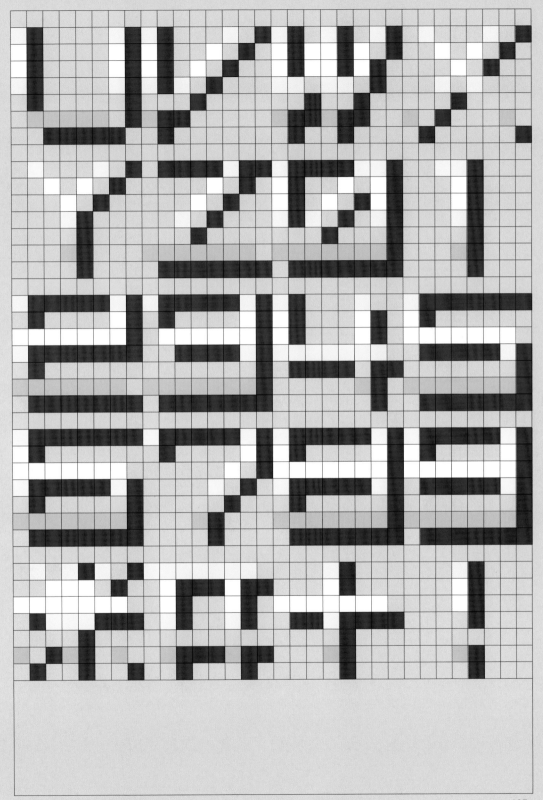

04

SERIF

MOUSE TRAP EXIDY/1981

Mouse Trap is a clone of *Pac-Man* (see page 24) featuring mice, dogs and cats. It has the second earliest serif face in the arcade, with a full character set, unlike *Comotion* (see page 110). The double serif on the I is interesting and not as distracting as its shape suggests.

TRIPLE PUNCH KKI/1982

A bearded carpenter who looks like Nintendo's Mario is chased by gorillas in *Triple Punch*...the setting seems to have been directly inspired by *Donkey Kong*, but the gameplay is original. The typeface is an early roman font, but the serifs are inconsistent and badly designed.

SPY HUNTER BALLY MIDWAY/1983

Inspired by James Bond cars, *Spy Hunter* was supposed to be a licensed game. The typeface is a roman, but the designer may have wanted a bit more action, as there is a slight slant to the right. Nearly every letter has something wrong with it, and for a franchise that skirted a movie series, the typography wasn't strong.

04 SERIF

EXERION JALECO/1983

A space shoot 'em up with realistic inertia in its controls, an element that didn't transfer to console ports. This serif face was derived from *Chameleon*, which was released by Jaleco the same year. Adding serifs to an already cramped design should pose a challenge, but the designers have avoided this problem by including them only occasionally. An unconventional decision was made about which serifs to keep on E and F.

WONDER PLANET DATA EAST/1987

A vertical cute 'em up from a developer that took pride in odd games, as echoed in the strange design here. Its black serif type doesn't look appropriate for the genre – maybe the designer was inspired by Cooper Black (Oswald Bruce Cooper, 1922)? The blunt deformation of letters like M, N and W, and just one pixel that distinguishes Q from O, are the highlights of the design. H, U and V need more thickness to harmonize with the other characters.

HEAVYWEIGHT CHAMP SEGA/1987

This seemingly shameless clone of *Punch-Out!!* (Nintendo, 1987) is actually a remake of Sega's original *Heavyweight Champ*, first released in 1976. The later version had unique motion control and involved a swivelling cabinet. It is unclear what aesthetic Sega was trying to achieve here, but it looks like a slightly slanted version of Cooper Black (as was used in the logo), with the texture of rusted steel. The use of four colours is complex and efficient.

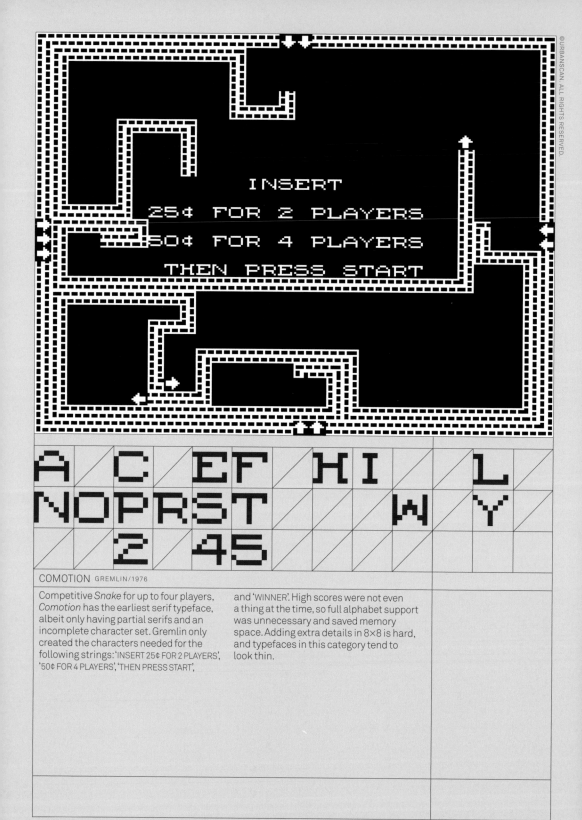

INSERT
25¢ FOR 2 PLAYERS
50¢ FOR 4 PLAYERS
THEN PRESS START

A C EF HI L
NOPRST W Y
2 45

COMOTION GREMLIN/1976

Competitive *Snake* for up to four players, *Comotion* has the earliest serif typeface, albeit only having partial serifs and an incomplete character set. Gremlin only created the characters needed for the following strings: 'INSERT 25¢ FOR 2 PLAYERS', '50¢ FOR 4 PLAYERS', 'THEN PRESS START',

and 'WINNER'. High scores were not even a thing at the time, so full alphabet support was unnecessary and saved memory space. Adding extra details in 8×8 is hard, and typefaces in this category tend to look thin.

KREDIT: 002	SPIELER: 1 24050	TOP ZAHL : 20000

Welche Staatsangehoerigkeit hat der Rennfahrer Alan Jones ?

richtige Antwort gibt **1750** Punkte

A. Die australische

B. Die neuseelaendische

C. Die englische

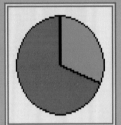

ABCDEFGHIJKLM
NOPQRSTUVWXYZ
abcdefghijklm
nopqrstuvwxyz
0123456789ÄÖß

QUIZMASTER LÖWEN SPIELAUTOMATEN/1985

Outside of the home and arcade environments, videogames could be found in pubs, taverns and drug stores in the form of quiz machines. This West German game from the pre-reunification era was made by Löwen Spielautomaten, a company that still thrives in the videogame industry. This serif typeface is well executed, especially in the lowercase department, where Japanese developers often struggled.

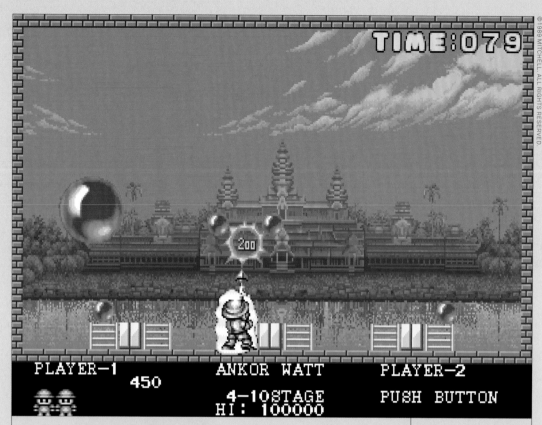

TIME:079

PLAYER-1
450

ANKOR WATT
4-10STAGE
HI: 100000

PLAYER-2
PUSH BUTTON

A B C D E F G H I J K L M
N O P Q R S T U V W X Y Z
a b c d e f g h i j k l m
n o p q r s t u v w x y z
0 1 2 3 4 5 6 7 8 9

PANG MITCHELL/1989

An action puzzle in which the player shoots bouncing balls, *Pang* is easy to understand and to play, and was followed by three sequels. The typeface is nicely done. Q is my favourite, because the tail appears to be broken up into an arc inside an O with a little detail protruding. That is probably not the original intention, but (mis)interpretation is part of the fun in analysing these typefaces.

DOUBLE AXLE TAITO/1991

The *Double Axle* typeface is loosely modelled on Quiz Show (see pages 18 and 44–45) with added serifs. This style of metallic gradation is distinctly American, as it reflects a blue sky and earthy landscape on shiny metal – fitting for a monster-truck racing game.

BLUE HAWK DOOYONG/1993

Blue Hawk is perhaps the most realistic game by Korean developer Dooyong. The typeface was originally created by Capcom in 1987 for use in *Black Tiger* and subsequently featured in a number of their games. A lowercase was added a year later in *LED Storm* and the most popular version featured in *Final Fight* (1989) and again in *Street Fighter II* (1991). The *Blue Hawk* typeface has almost identical base letterforms to Capcom's font, with the exception of C, G, H and R.

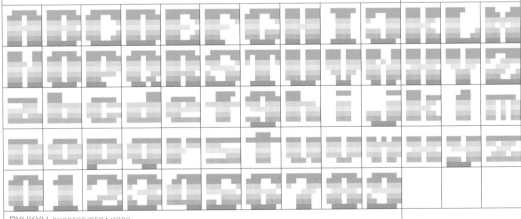

NINJA GAIDEN TECMO/1988

The famous ninja series started off as a cooperative beat 'em up in which players used their fists more than their swords, but it has since been discarded from the series chronology. The typography started off with a slightly expanded roman that was vertically condensed to be more accurate. It is a nice design, but has some issues with horizontal proportion due to the inconsistent inclusion of serifs, such as the wide A and narrow R. Not a unique typeface, but not a bad one either.

RYUKYU SUCCESS/SEGA/1990

Ryukyu is named after a group of islands off the southwest coast of Japan. However, the game itself doesn't have much to do with island life, being a puzzler in which players must line up cards. The typeface is only partially serif, but it tries to put in as many serifs and beaks as possible, even in the J and numerals. The M and W compress details wonderfully. The lowercase accommodates descenders by shifting the baseline.

USAAF MUSTANG NMK/1990

A horizontal World War II shoot 'em up developed by NMK in which the player pilots a USAAF P-51 Mustang against German and Japanese opposition, starting in Spain. Although this is not a great typeface overall, the mid-tone pixel within the G allows the crossbar to touch the stem while giving it a space at the same time, which is absolute genius.

PLAY GIRLS HOT-B./1992

This pornographic version of *Arkanoid* (Taito, 1986) uses a serif typeface with unusual placement of thick stems. The flipped Z could be dismissed as a mistake, but I find it to be unintentionally brilliant because there are so many words spelled with an S but pronounced with a Z or vice versa. When you don't know which letter to use, this S-like Z can actually be very handy. It could also be a substitute to the German ß (Eszett).

POWER INSTINCT ATLUS/1993

A fairly standard fighting game, except that all of its characters are related – with some exceptions in later games in the series. *Power Instinct* followed a videogame tradition of using a yellow bold slab serif, and the sequels change things up. The series as a whole has an interesting family of slab designs that never matured. The base letterform here is OK, but the shadow layer has no manual correction and flickers during play.

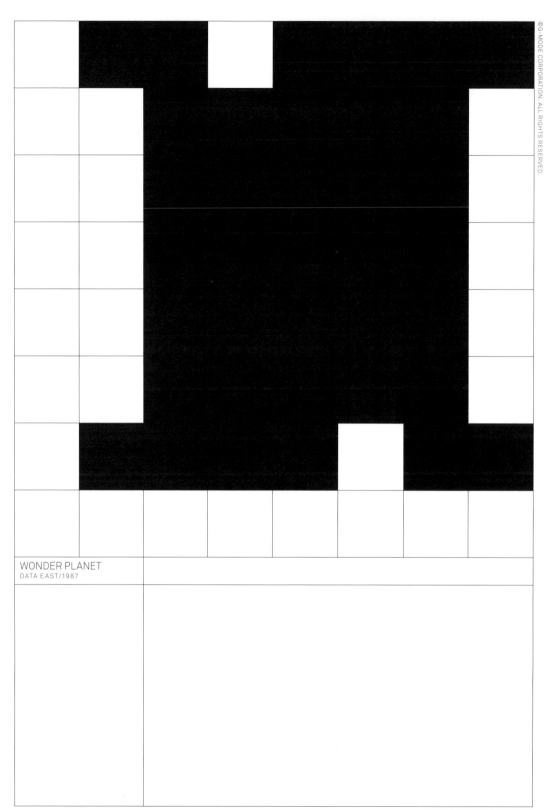

WONDER PLANET
DATA EAST/1987

PLAY GIRLS
HOT-B./1992

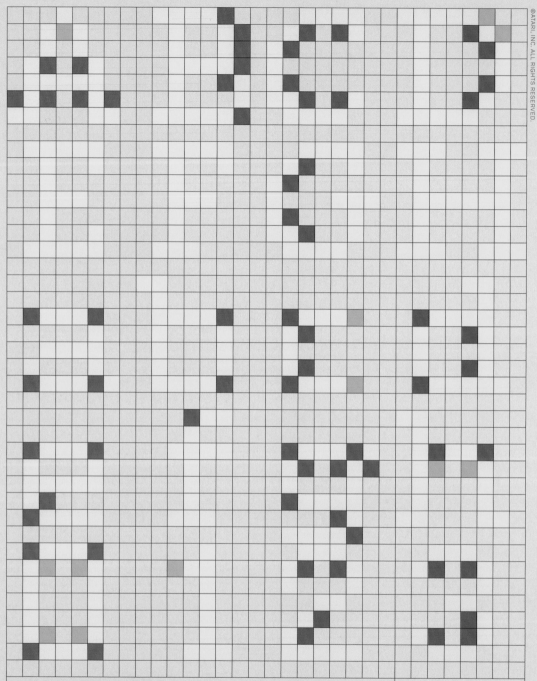

KLAX ATARI GAMES/1989

A puzzle game in which you line up coloured blocks, similar to *Columns* (see page 188). *Klax* is one of only a few arcade games to include both italic and bold as well as regular typefaces.

The sans italic isn't a traditional match for the serif roman, but it is functional. The bold is not two full pixels thick, so it feels more like a semibold. J and T are oddly positioned.

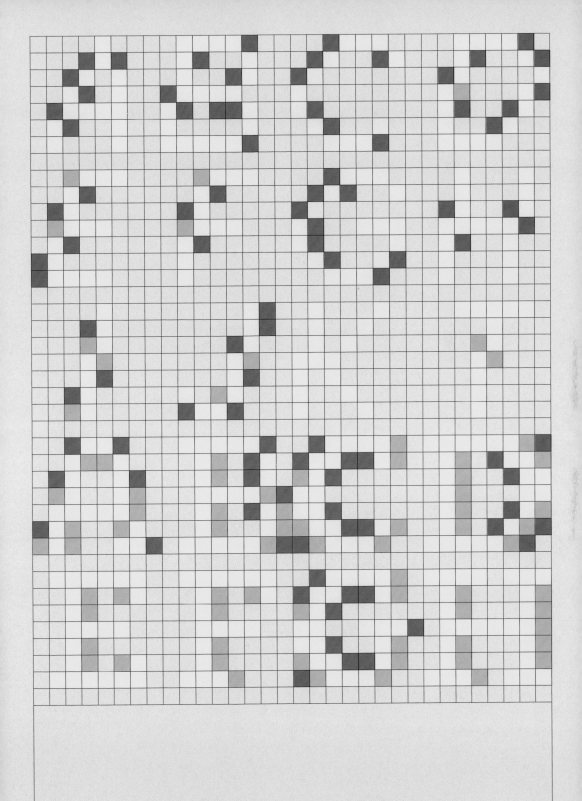

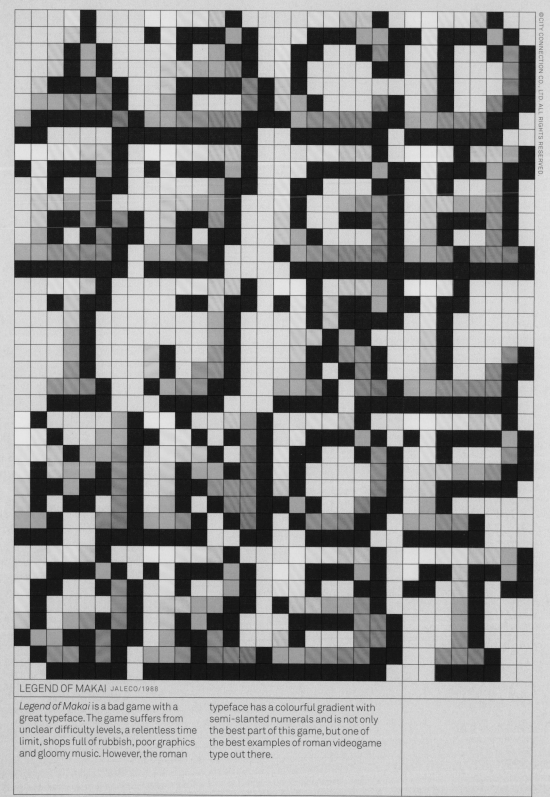

LEGEND OF MAKAI JALECO/1988

Legend of Makai is a bad game with a great typeface. The game suffers from unclear difficulty levels, a relentless time limit, shops full of rubbish, poor graphics and gloomy music. However, the roman typeface has a colourful gradient with semi-slanted numerals and is not only the best part of this game, but one of the best examples of roman videogame type out there.

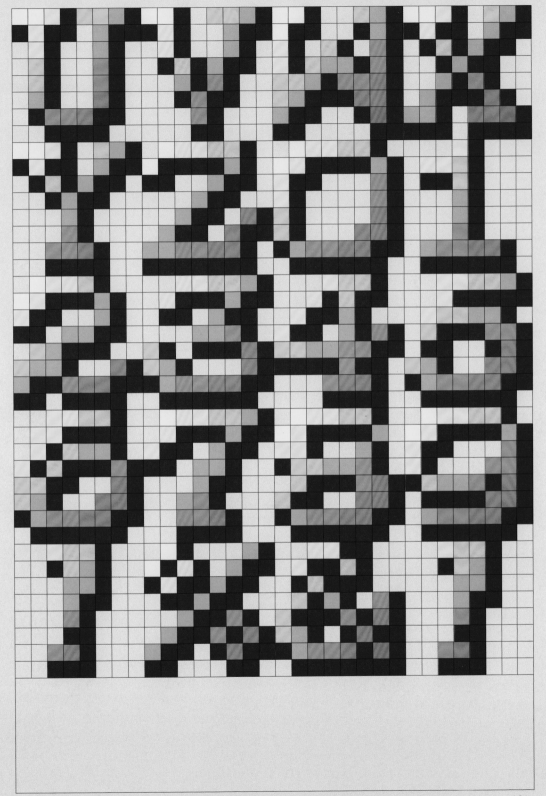

SUPER SPACEFORTRESS MACROSS II BANPRESTO/1993

A horizontal shooter game in which players can transform from fighter jet to humanoid robot, just like the characters in the anime television series *Macross*. The typeface above was used in the first game, with the addition here of mid-tone colours in characters B, C, D, E and F. The use of a mid-tone colour to anti-alias is effective, and the ink traps of M and N are particularly notable. The Q, however, is quite a messy design.

GUMBO MIN CORP./1994

Min Corp. was a Korean developer of adult puzzle games. The Gumbo typeface appears in all six of the company's games, and has been taken from Capcom's *Captain Commando* (1991). The lowercase height is unnatural, but Capcom improved this in their later games. In this version of the face, the gradation of lavender and cyan is striking against the dark background.

GOLDEN AXE: THE DUEL SEGA/1994

Golden Axe was a popular fantasy beat 'em up game series. Most games in the series were scrolling beat 'em ups, but this particular instalment featured versus-mode sword fighting instead. The graphics are great, and so is the typeface – a serif face with swashes and mid-stem spikes. The only element that doesn't work is the inclusion of grey pixels as the mid-tone colour used for anti-aliasing.

POWER INSTINCT LEGENDS ATLUS/CAVE/1995

This typeface is loosely based on a slab roman font. However, it is clear the designer was playing around with the traditional style to create a fun and unusual typeface. Whether through naivety or a disregard for the basics, the designer's choices have nonetheless worked to the typeface's advantage, helping it to stand out. The Q, for example, has a massive tail that sacrifices thickness on the oval stroke and is thus both terrible and awesome.

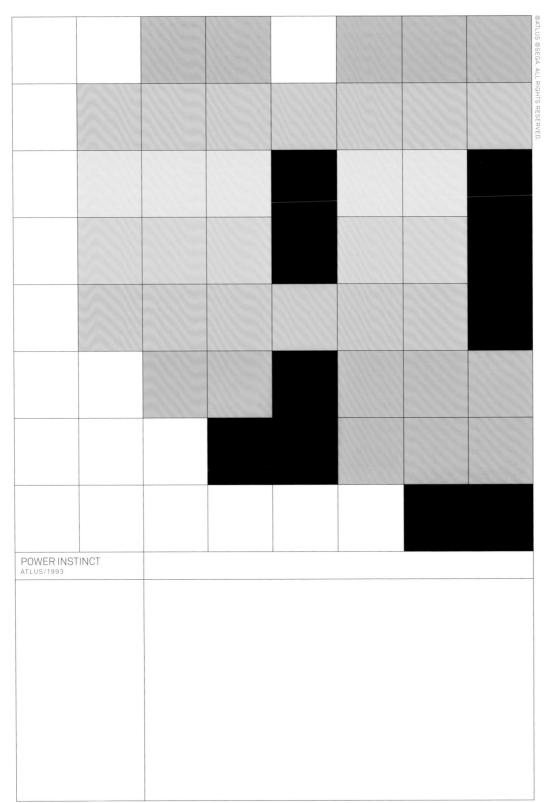

POWER INSTINCT
ATLUS/1993

HEAVEN'S GATE
ATLUS/RACDYM/1996

POWER INSTINCT LEGENDS ATLUS/CAVE/1995

There is something adorable about the *Power Instinct* franchise. The developers made three attempts at creating a fat and comical slab typeface, but the style and legibility of the font never really improved. The result was a set of unique but mediocre typefaces, all three of which should be dismissed as bad fonts on a practical level. However, they have a certain charm that is difficult to disregard.

PLAYER SELECT

12

NAME	SHINDO JIN
AGE	21
SEX	MALE
NATIONALITY	JAPAN
SPECIALITY	UNKNOWN
LINEAGE	UNKNOWN

JIN

Credits 3

ABCDEFGH IJKLM
NOPQRSTU VWXYZ
abcdefgh ij&lm
nopqrs tu vwxyz
0123456789

HEAVEN'S GATE ATLUS/RACDYM/1996

A 3D fighting game that has now largely been forgotten. The serif typeface is helped by appealing colour choices, however, there is a lot left to be desired in the letterforms and the use of shadows is ineffective. The use of high waists in B, E and S is an interesting idea but is applied with more confidence in the numbers. The lowercase has a sloped top serif, but the illegible p and q stand testament to the fact that over-cropping can lead to illegible characters.

05

MICR

MICR

Magnetic Ink Character Recognition (MICR) is a printing technology invented in the United States in the 50s. It uses ink containing magnetic iron oxide and a very mechanical numeric typeface that allows the characters to be read by both the human eye and magnetic scanners.

MICR was intended to speed up bank operations by processing numbers mechanically and was used for bank cheques and documents of a similar nature. The peculiar design of the numerals attracted the attention of graphic and typeface designers – to them, it was more than just a financial convenience.

A typeface called Westminster was one of the earliest to sport such aesthetics. In around 1964, the London designer Leo Maggs was asked to draw an article title in a futuristic style for a magazine. He used the MICR typeface as his inspiration, and later he expanded the character set and submitted it to Letraset, the largest photo-typesetting sheet manufacturer.

Letraset rejected the design, so Maggs took it to Photoscript Ltd, who released it as Westminster. Five years later, Letraset released Data 70 (Bob Newman, 1970) as a response to Westminster, which had proven popular. There were others, too: Gemini, also known as Automation, Gemini Computer or Sonic, depending on the publisher (designer unknown, c. 1965); Moore Computer (David Moore, 1968); and Orbit-B (Stan Biggenden, 1972).

No type classification system lists MICR as its own category. In videogames, however, the sheer number of MICR-based pixel typefaces demands a dedicated section. In games where science, the future, outer space, aliens and machines were ubiquitous, MICR typefaces were a perfect fit. They were used most often in shoot 'em ups, but sometimes showed up in unexpected contexts, such as football or Mahjong games.

MICR typefaces started appearing in arcades in 1981, as in *Strategy X* (Konami, overleaf), *Turtles* (Konami, also known as *Turpin* and published by Sega, overleaf) and *Space Odyssey* (Sega). The square nature of the design behaved well on a pixel grid, without trying too hard to retain its unorthodox placement of stem thicknesses. Almost all the new designs appear to have been based on Data 70, probably due to its popularity. It stimulated Japanese developers' creativity and the number of unique designs proceeded to rise. It was almost as though Japan's designers enjoyed working with Latin type, and the creative possibilities it offered, more than with the Japanese script.

Another important and unique take on the MICR style was found in Namco's *Xevious* (1982, see page 48), which was mixed with Amelia.*

MICR was more or less extinct by the end of the 90s, and only a few games carried on the tradition. The industry had moved on and learned the art of subtlety, no longer relying on wacky details that screamed 'Future!' But the appetite for mechanical-looking typefaces has never gone away, and in modern games typefaces such as DIN, Eurostile, Bank Gothic and similar square designs are commonplace. Today, our tastes have changed and Westminster and Data 70 are considered retro, but we shouldn't forget to respect these elders that were once the face of the future.

* A typeface released in 1967 that was designed by Stan Davis, published by VGC and loosely based on the MICR category. It was made famous by its use on the cover of The Beatles' *Yellow Submarine*.

MICR

1234567890

WESTMINSTER

ABCDEFGHIJKLMN
OPQRSTUVWXYZ
abcdefghijklmn
opqrstuvwxyz
1234567890

DATA 70

ABCDEFGHJKLMN
OPQRSTUVWXYZ
abcdefghijklmn
opqrstuvwxyz
1234567890

STRATEGY X KONAMI/1981

This tank-based shoot 'em up was among the first to bring MICR design to videogame typography. Compared to *Turtles* (below), this typeface has a more complete character set, with rounded corners, suggesting that *Strategy X* uses a later design. The rounded corners make the font more legible and are therefore an effective deviation from the squared nature of the original style.

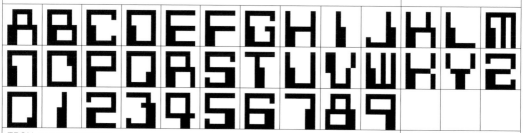

TURTLES KONAMI/1981

Despite having a similar name, *Turtles* has nothing to do with the *Teenage Mutant Ninja Turtles* (see page 34). This maze-running game features a turtle that sneaks into a building in order to rescue its family. Konami released two games in 1981 featuring different interpretations of Data 70 (the other being *Strategy X*), but I could not track down their precise release dates. Judging by the incomplete character set here and a less polished design in comparison to *Strategy X*, this seems to be the first Data 70 adaptation ever, at least in Japan.

TRON BALLY MIDWAY/1982

Tron inspired many videogame designers when it hit cinema screens in 1982, and Bally Midway was no exception. Although the film itself did not use a MICR typeface, this almost perfect adaptation of Data 70, with some minor deviations in Q, 0 and 3, felt right at home in the game.

A.D. 2083 MIDCOIN/1983

A bi-directional side-scrolling shooter game in which a space shuttle shoots down enemy starships reminiscent of the TIE fighters from Star Wars. There are a few possible names to which this font could be attributed – programmers Alberto Troiano or Maurizio Tesorone, who assumed various roles at Midcoin, or perhaps graphic and sound artist Tullio Tesorone. The typeface was a liberal adaptation of Data 70, with some inconsistencies.

GROBDA NAMCO/1984

Namco took up the challenge of making a bold MICR typeface in *Grobda*, and the result is quite convincing. The weight distribution of Data 70 caps make for a better bold than that of Westminster.

The difficulty to distinguish between 4 and 9 is a recurring issue in the MICR genre, but *Grobda* managed to avoid this by adding a slope to one of these problematic characters.

SPACE POSITION NASCO/SEGA/1986

A futuristic racing game in which players can fly but, in doing so, they lose fuel. The fuel is your lifeforce, and you also lose some upon crashing. Slanted Data 70 combines the concepts of 'future' and 'speed' perfectly in one typeface. Instead of placing a thick stem inside each character, the designer has moved it to the outside. It's a simple and clever italic trick.

MUTANT NIGHT UPL/KAWAKUS/1987

A run-and-gun game in which the player character has a large eyeball instead of a head. This adaptation of Data 70 introduces middle thickness, making for a less jarring design. It was a clever improvement upon previous versions but was hardly used in later games. The developer, UPL, seemed to favour bold and contrasted sans, so this typeface might have been too safe for them.

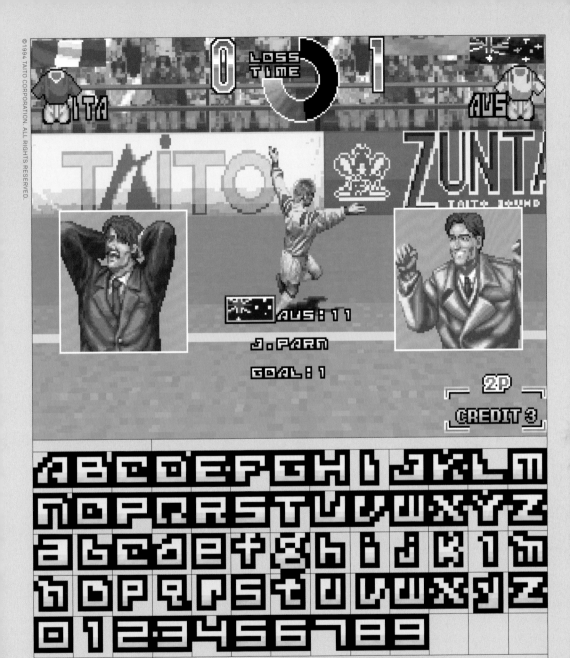

TAITO POWER GOAL   TAITO/1994

This is the fourth and final game in the *Hat Trick Hero* franchise. *Taito Cup Finals*, the previous instalment in the series, used the Ray Force font (see pages 142–43) for player names, but with different gradation.

In this game, a new lowercase was added that does not draw from any existing MICR typeface. It diverges from traditional type design, and even mundane letters such as b, n and q are surprisingly original.

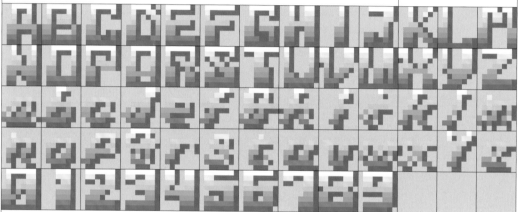

ALPHA ONE VISION ELECTRONICS/1988

A horizontal shooting game made in Australia by Kyle Hodgetts and Tony Windsor. It is likely that Hodgetts designed the typeface, as he continued to make similar games by himself using similar fonts. The rather cool MICR typeface employs the same slanting technique seen in *Space Position* (see page 133), though inconsistently, and the wide M and W are also visually jarring.

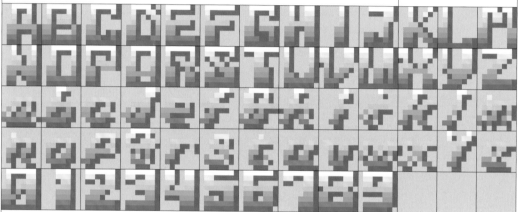

THUNDER CROSS II KONAMI/1991

This sequel to *Thunder Cross* has a very tenuous, and somewhat pointless, plot: the enemies from the previous game have come back to life and players need to defeat them all over again. The Data 70-esque caps and numerals are recycled from the first game, but the lowercase is new. It is unclear as to why the designer made a cursive italic typeface like this – perhaps it is the unintentional brilliance of experimentation. The lowercase never appears in the game though.

STEEL GUNNER 2 NAMCO/1991

A sci-fi shooter with mounted light guns. While the first *Steel Gunner* game used the *Pac-Man* typeface (see page 24), as most Namco titles did, this sequel uses a unique font of its own. In true Namco fashion, as seen in *Xevious* (see page 48), the distribution of weight is unconventional. The top right corner of the T, for example, is very heavy in comparison to the opposite corner.

F-1 GRAND PRIX PART II VIDEO SYSTEM CO./1992

Video System Co.'s *F-1 Grand Prix* games came at the height of Formula 1's popularity in Japan. The games featured an amazing theme song as well as actual teams and drivers, including the legendary Ayrton Senna. The typeface used to show the racing-car specifications is a liberal adaptation of MICR, especially in the numerals and lowercase. The M and N need improvement.

ZED BLADE NMK/1994

A horizontal shoot 'em up with a 90s disco-style title screen. The typeface has an interesting take on the thick stems of Data 70, in which a grey tone works as a half thickness. Overall this is a very faithful adaptation of Data 70. It goes to show how many different solutions can be found to one problem.

SPACE POSITION
NASCO/SEGA/1986

STEEL GUNNER 2
NAMCO/1991

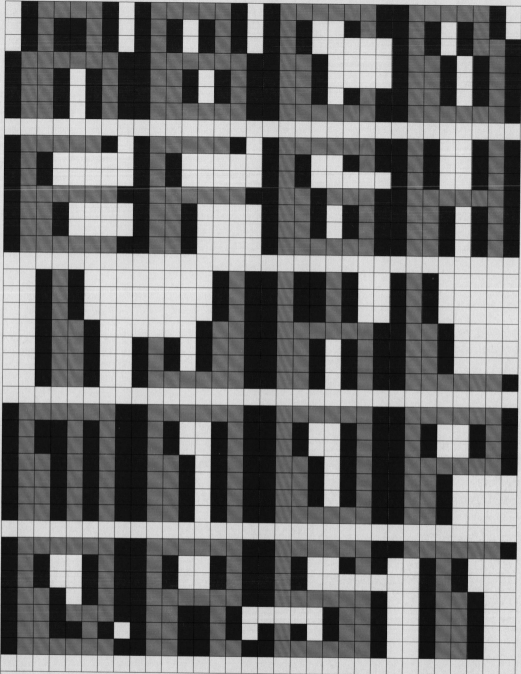

OUTFOXIES NAMCO/1994

Three of the seven typefaces used in *Outfoxies* were MICR-based. The typeface pictured above and opposite was the most prominent of these faces. The outline creates a blurred effect that simulates a low-quality CRT or VHS tape. In the other MICR designs for the game, one uses only a single colour without outlines, and the second has interlaced stripes and comes with a lowercase, despite only being used for the phrase GAME OVER. For an example not based on MICR, see page 98.

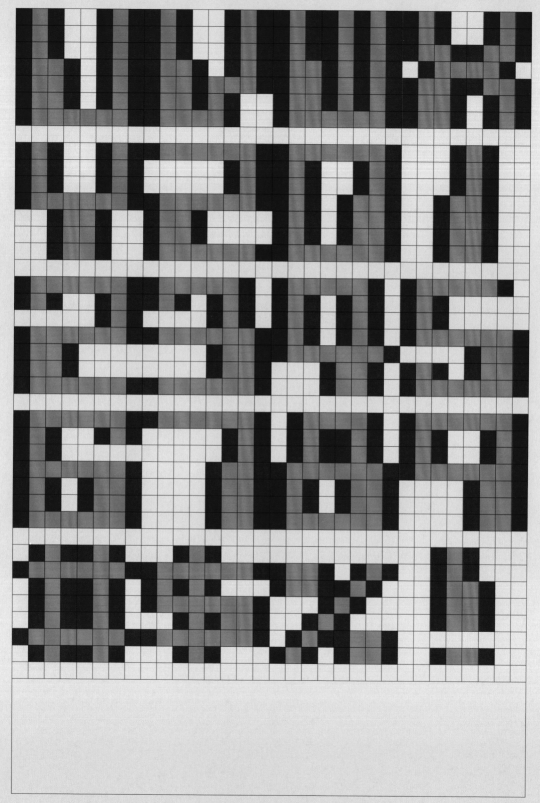

RAY FORCE TAITO/1993

The *Ray Force* typeface is a masterpiece. A slick Data 70 adaptation with an alternating colour palette that creates an interlacing effect – *Ray Force* uses the CRT screen vertically, so the interlace also moves vertically. No other typeface demands to be seen in motion as much as this one and a static depiction can't fully do it justice. It is an incredible technical achievement.

FIXEIGHT TOAPLAN/1992

Eight imprisoned warriors are promised a pardon if they agree to take on an invader from another dimension. The *Fixeight* typeface is a solid example of how to adapt MICR for a bold monospaced design.

The M and W are notable diversions from the Data 70 model. The distinction between I and 1 is effective, but it is difficult to tell the difference between between Q and 0.

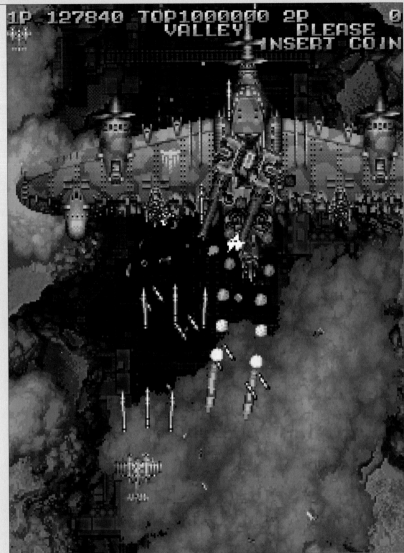

BATTLE GAREGGA – TYPE 2 RAIZING/EIGHTING/1996

Battle Garegga is now considered to be a classic game due to its adaptive difficulty levels, intricate pixel art and soundtrack. The capital letters are a mixture of Quiz Show (see pages 18 and 44–45) and the MICR genre.

The jump between thicknesses works as a nice little accent. The spiritual sequel, *Armed Police Batrider* (Eighting, 1998), uses the same typeface but with horizontal gradation.

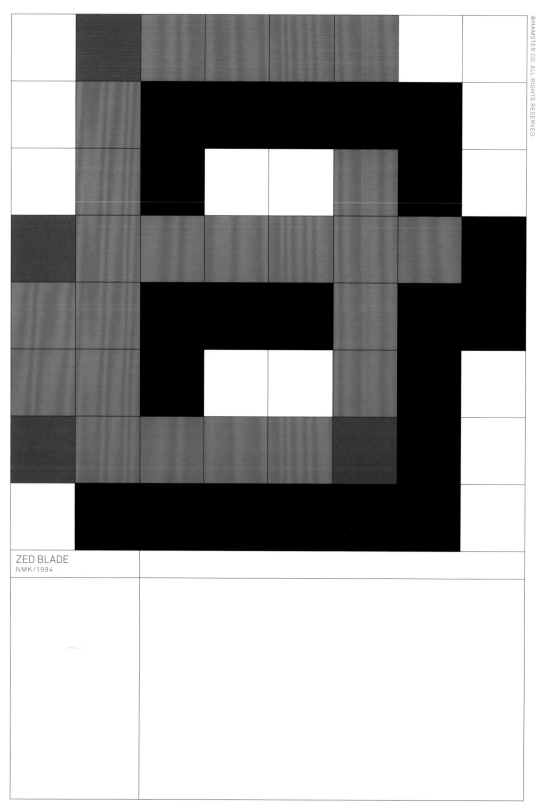

ZED BLADE
NMK/1994

BATTLE GAREGGA
RAIZING/EIGHTING/1996

06

SLANTED

KRULL GOTTLIEB/1983

This arcade adaptation does a fairly good job of representing the (terribly underrated) 1983 film. The italic typeface is the game's own invention, and is well designed for a single-colour face with no mid-tone pixels. It is only half-slanted though, as most letters have right-side uprights and only slant to the left. The numerals were less successful.

TIME PILOT '84 KONAMI/1984

This sequel to the 1982 sci-fi shooter *Time Pilot* comes with more detailed graphics and its own typeface, whereas the first game used the *Pac-Man* (see page 24) variant of Quiz Show (see pages 18 and 44–45). An early example of a successful set of italics in single colour, extending the top strokes to fill space and add character to the design. The typeface was also used in *Contra* (Konami, 1987).

KONAMI GT KONAMI/1985

A first-person driving game. The typeface is a bold version of that used in *Time Pilot '84* (above). To make a bold italic work well in a single colour is a feasible but daunting task in the first place, but making the stems four pixels wide is too much. The designer of this typeface could not handle the challenge, and the result is a collection of unpolished and inconsistent letters.

BLACK PANTHER KONAMI/1987

A side-scrolling beat 'em up in which players control a robotic panther. The typeface used in the game is unusual in that all of the colour-based detail is applied to the extrusion, and the effect is rather photographic.

Unfortunately the base letterforms are not polished, horrible in fact. The creative merit in this typeface lies mostly in the gradation effect. The leftward tail of Q adds extra slant.

BATTLECRY HOME DATA/1991

Both of the fonts here come from the same mediocre fighting game, made by a company previously focused on producing pornographic Mahjong. The first typeface, probably an early version of the second design, does not seem to appear in the game. The second typeface is displayed on the results screen after each stage. In both, letters look more shaky than slanted, as though you are looking at a mirage.

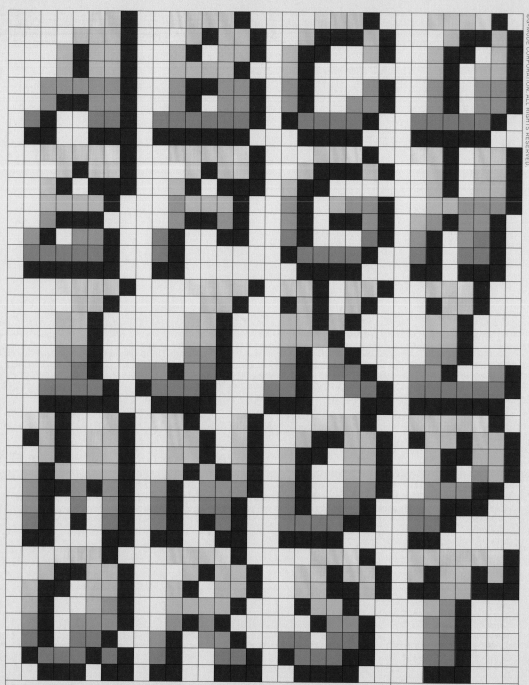

THE CLIFFHANGER: EDWARD RANDY DATA EAST/1990

A steampunk side-scroller inspired by action films, especially *Indiana Jones*. In turn, Treasure's *Gunstar Heroes* (1993) and *Guardian Heroes* (1996) took inspiration from this game. The slanted semi-serif typeface is not particularly well-drawn, judging by the letterforms alone. Many characters lack thickness and the slanting is not applied consistently. These negative elements, however, are made up for by the popping colour choice of yellow, green and purple.

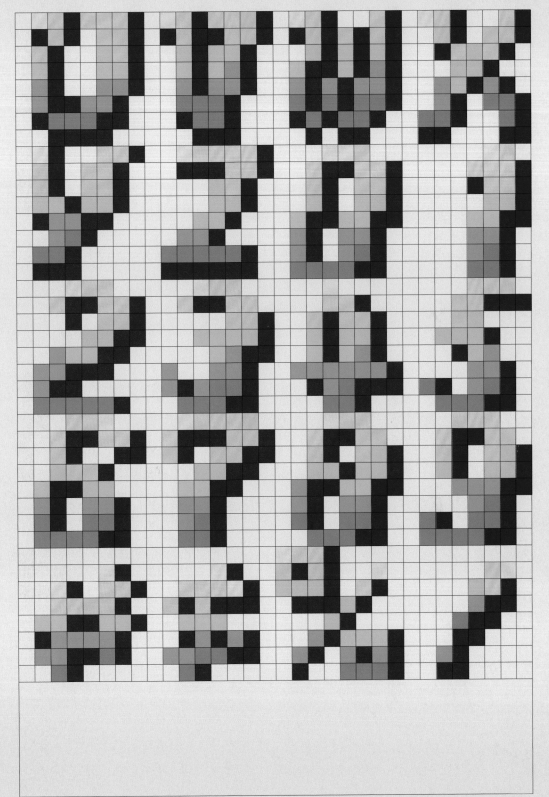

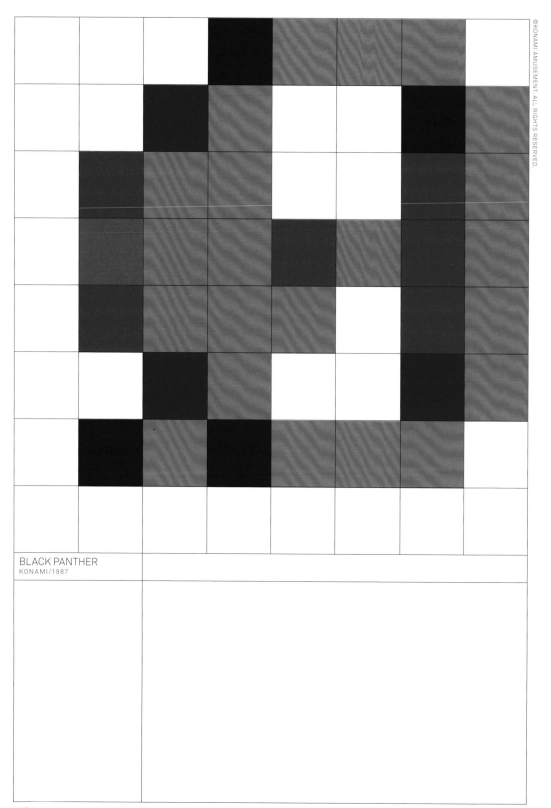

BLACK PANTHER
KONAMI/1987

SALAMANDER 2
KONAMI/1996

GONDOMANIA DATA EAST/1987

It can be difficult to create slanted typefaces in a limited amount of space without jagged edges appearing in every letter. This fantasy vertical shooter, however, overcomes these issues by anti-aliasing with a second colour.

The strokes generally get thicker at the bottom, which is expressed in the colours of the top and bottom tips (see the top right and bottom left of I). Achieving this level of subtlety with only two colours is seriously impressive.

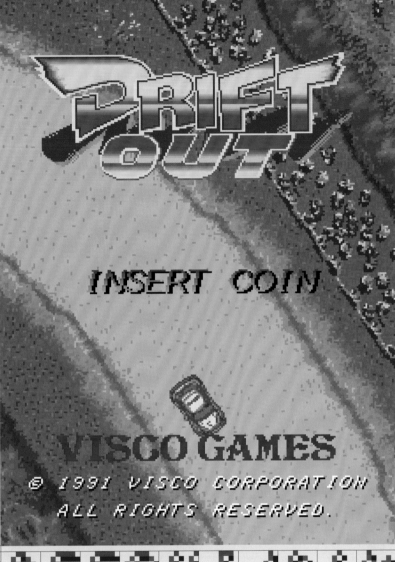

INSERT COIN

VISCO GAMES

© 1991 VISCO CORPORATION
ALL RIGHTS RESERVED.

DRIFT OUT VISCO/1991

This typeface for the top-down rally game *Drift Out* is superbly executed. The subtle personality of the letterforms is achieved through the trimming of top-right corners in letters such as K, M, N, U, V and W, which could otherwise have been cut to maintain the slant angle. The shadow is a 1×1 shift to the bottom right with some manual correction, but does not always follow this rule, as in I.

· SEGA 1988 ·

one day, suoy was playing with
her pets bin and pin in
a beautiful flower garden.

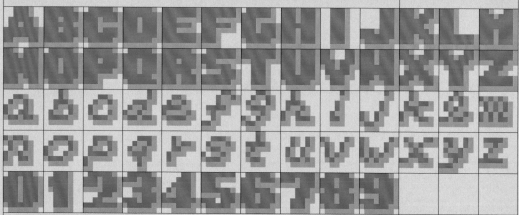

DYNAMITE DÜX SEGA/1988

Behind Mario, Sonic and Crash are
many forgotten mascots. One of these
is *Dynamite Düx*, created by none other
than game designer Yu Suzuki, who also
designed *Space Harrier*, *Out Run* and
After Burner (see pages 30, 62 and 219).
The font's capitals, used for the end

credits, seem to be derived from *After
Burner* (see page 62), an earlier game
also designed by Suzuki. The lowercase
is a crisply pixelated cursive with a fragile
appearance helped by the inclusion of
a shadow layer. The g is not as compact
as the other descending letters.

NAME—Carl·F·Graystone

CLASS—Knight

SEX—Male

ALIGNMENT—Lawful Good

AGE—26

HEIGHT—77in

WEIGHT—195lb

HAIR—Gold

EYES—Brown

BLOODTYPE—A

STAR—Aries

WEAPON—Morning Star

DARK SEAL DATA EAST/1990

A slanted font uses up more horizontal space than an upright one, as does a serif design compared to sans. Any typeface that does both is therefore a rarity. You might see Renaissance books using upright caps mixed with italic lowercase, but not the other way around, as in *Dark Seal*. The letters are well-formed, but the combination of styles looks strange.

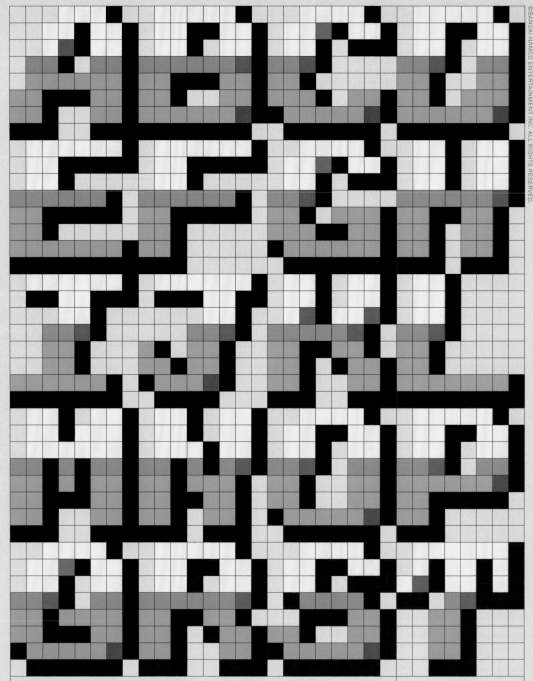

MACH BREAKERS: NUMAN ATHLETICS 2 NAMCO/1995

In *Mach Breakers*, superhuman athletes compete in a dozen insane events, such as javelin-throwing with missiles. Namco generally used the font originally seen in *Pac-Man* (see page 24), and the intention here could be a dynamic slanted version in line with the sporting theme. The typeface includes eight colours, and half of them are used for anti-aliasing achieving a visual sweet spot somewhere between jagged and blurred.

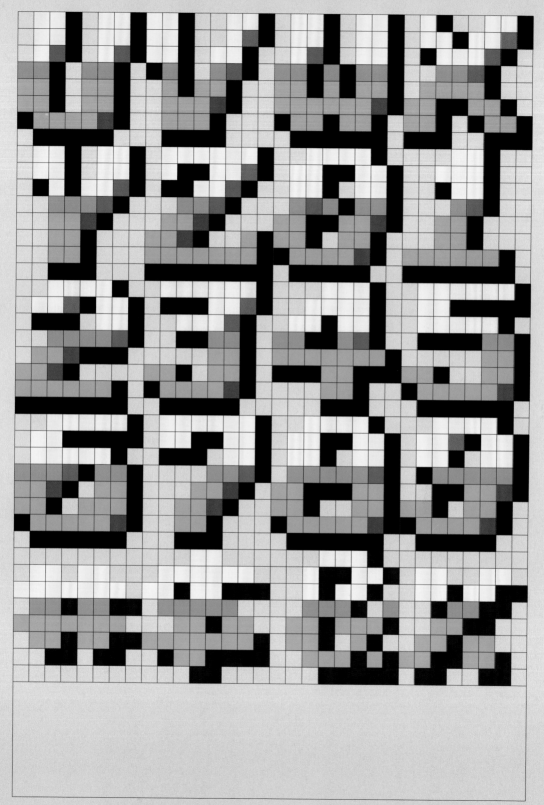

SUPER MONACO GP SEGA/1989

The track featured in this racing game is not an accurate depiction of the Circuit de Monaco, it's more like Japan's Suzuka Circuit with Monaco's geography. The rather obtrusive typography uses an appropriately styled slanted sans with a slight emboss effect. Some letters, D and H for example, are too narrow and would have benefited from a gentler slant angle.

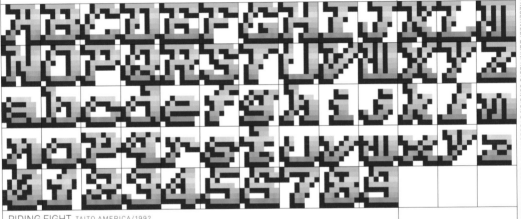

RIDING FIGHT TAITO AMERICA/1992

Taito have attempted to tackle the difficult challenge of combining italics, serifs and a bold style in their typeface design for this hoverboard *Road Rash* (Electronic Arts, 1991) clone. Sadly, given the inconsistent stem thicknesses and messy lowercase design, the typeface is not quite a success. It does, however, convey a strong sense of speed through its use of long in-strokes and horizontal gradation.

ULTRA TOUKON DENSETSU BANPRESTO + TSUBURAYA PROD./1993

The *Ultraman* television franchise that inspired *Ultra Toukon Densetsu* remained largely exclusive to Japan. This beat 'em up game features comical mutant 'Ultramen', and the puffy typeface sits in contrast to the more serious tone of the TV series. The resulting font struggles a bit in execution, but overall is very well done. The 16×16 version is a similar design, but upright and differently textured.

ULTRA X WEAPONS BANPRESTO/TSUBURAYA PROD./1995

A vertical shooter based on the television series *Ultraman*. Players must pilot a fighter jet, occasionally helped by Ultra Heroes. The game uses photorealistic 3D sources and anti-aliasing. This brassy typeface looks as if it was computer-rendered and then finished by hand. Overcoming the difficulty of creating slanted letters with a good command of colour, this is one of the most technically impressive italic typefaces in the arcade.

SALAMANDER 2 KONAMI/1996

A set of upright capitals with an italic lowercase is considered to be a traditional combination in typography. Examples of this can be seen in *Dynamite Düx* (see page 158) and *Thunder Cross II* (see page 136). This primary *Salamander 2* typeface (see page 99 for the secondary typeface), however, reverses the style by having an italic uppercase and an upright lowercase. The lowercase has been recycled from the design for the original game. The seriffed capitals are reminiscent of those used in *Time Pilot '84* (see page 150) and *Contra* (Konami, 1987), and work well apart from Y, which is distinct from the V in the font, but confusing without comparison.

TIME PILOT '84
KONAMI/1984

BATTLECRY
HOME DATA/1991

HACHA MECHA FIGHTER NMK/1991

This animal-themed horizontal cute 'em up showcases the developer's obsession with character animation. In terms of the typography, both the 16×16 font used for the logo and the 8×8 font pictured above are colourful italic faces. Despite some character height alignment issues in the lowercase, this is a consistent and cute typeface. The lilac to yellow to white gradation reflects the themes in the game. The Japanese character set is shown overleaf.

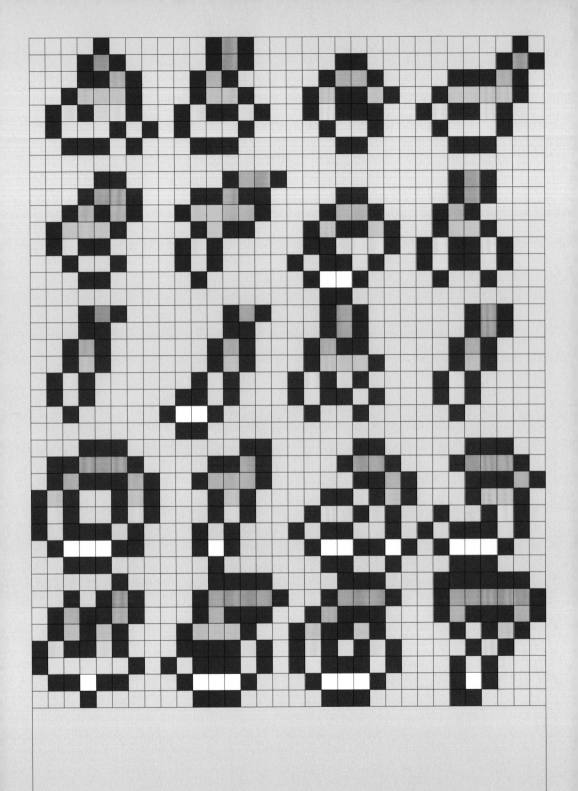

HACHA MECHA FIGHTER NMK/1991

MASTERBOY *de* BRONCE

EMPOLLON

*SCORE: *51100*

*NOTA : *5.40*

SOLITARIO

*SCORE: *54000*

*NOTA : *5.40*

DONATELLO

*SCORE: *65100*

*NOTA : *5.50*

DOBLES

*SCORE: *89900*

*NOTA : *5.70*

MASTER BOY GAELCO/1991

As far as quiz games go, *Master Boy* is not particularly noteworthy. Its typeface, however, is very interesting. The letters are slanted at a seemingly impossible angle, resulting in a design space that feels wider than 8×8 pixels. The strokes at the top left give the typeface a feeling of speed but may have been added simply to fill space. Cramming all of the details for M and W in without compromise, and still managing to make the characters slant this much, is an achievement.

MAHJONG ANGEL KISS JALECO/1995

The italic typeface in this pornographic Mahjong game is not bad, and the anti-aliasing is effective. However, this face design demonstrates the inherent challenge in applying a slant on one side only, which can make characters look triangular if not corrected. The x-height is initially 5px, but after drawing p and q a pixel taller, the designer appears to forget this rule.

PECULIAR CHARACTERS

Driven by the particular demands of the medium, arcade-game typefaces had to achieve a lot within an extremely limited format. Despite the shortcomings of the 8×8 typographic canvas, artists managed to create intricate and complex supplementary 'glyph' characters, many of which are unique to the world of videogames.

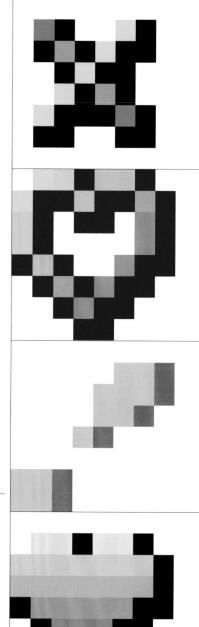

Unless they are text-heavy quizzes, videogames do not usually need more than letters, numbers and basic punctuation. Sometimes even the alphabet set is left incomplete because developers knew certain letters would not appear in the game and they wanted to save memory. The ASCII set* became common, and developers added whichever further characters they deemed necessary. These included Japanese *kana*, accented Latin letters, playing-card symbols and the Roman numerals I and II to indicate the game's players.

The copyright symbol was frequently used on the title screen, but the sound recording copyright symbol (℗) was used more frequently in earlier games, perhaps as an attempt to copyright the game product as audio, since, in their infancy, copyright law did not protect videogames. The @ sign was often useless in videogames and its ASCII slot ended up being filled with ©.

The grave accent (`) was included in ASCII for two purposes: literally as an accent (à), or as an opening quotation mark when curly typographers' quotes were not available. Japanese game developers must have thought it was an opening quotation mark, too, because there are many fonts that use it as a closing quotation mark, flipped horizontally.**

A couple of peculiar characters show up frequently in arcade game fonts and nowhere else: RUB and

END. In natural English, they are the delete and confirm buttons for the leaderboard entry screen. My theory for why RUB was chosen for character deletion is that the Japanese developers used the first three letters of the word 'rubber', the British word for a pencil eraser. Alternatively, there was BS for backspace, RV for reverse, and DEL, DL or a left-facing arrow for delete. The END symbol was also sometimes ED, OK or the carriage-return symbol.

What is fascinating about RUB and END is that three letters are crammed into 8×8 pixels. *Cue Brick* (Konami, 1989) even managed to fit EXIT into this canvas. There are all kinds of tricks used in such glyphs, from making a ligature form of END, to shifting baselines, to colouring each letter differently.

* A standard from 1963, short for American Standard Code for Information Interchange, which holds 93 visible characters and some invisible control characters, such as line break: !"#$%&'()*+,-./0123456789:;<=>?@ABCDEFGHIJKLMNOPQRSTUVWXYZ[\]^_`abcdefghijklmnopqrstuvwxyz{|}

** People still use ` today as a quotation mark or apostrophe and it is clearly intended to serve this double purpose, because it's readily available on English keyboard layouts. Today, we have curly typographer's quotation marks as separate Unicode characters: '' "".

07

CALLIGRAPHY & LETTERING

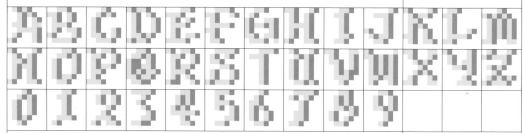

VENTURE EXIDY/1981

An adventure game in which players control a red smiley-face character who collects treasure. The game uses a set of very unusual medieval-style letters called Lombardic capitals. It is one of the most creative typefaces made in 1981 alongside the italic face used in *Mariner* (see page 178). It captures the highly calligraphic nature of Lombardic capitals very well and the designer has managed to compress lots of complex detail into each pixel.

KIKI KAIKAI TAITO/1986

A shooter game based on Japanese horror stories. Western developers have often created 'wonton' fonts (typefaces with contrived oriental features), but Japanese developers know better. Fonts in ninja or samurai games are known for their quick and punchy brush strokes, but here the typeface is 'written' with slowly twisting lines, evoking an eerie atmosphere.

CAPTAIN SILVER DATA EAST/1987

A side-scrolling, pirate-themed action game. *Captain Silver* is famous for having one of the most fragile player characters in game history – anything can kill you with one touch. This font succeeds in looking like the scribbled and faded handwriting one might expect to see on a pirate's map. Amongst the collection of wobbly letterforms, the symmetric X stands upright.

07 CALLIGRAPHY & LETTERING

PSYCHIC 5 JALECO/1987

A 2D platformer with five characters who have psychic powers – this game truly is a hidden gem. The letterforms have been created in a wispy Art Nouveau style to complement the supernatural theme.

There is not much logic or consistency in the application of the curled detailing, and it does not translate to a higher-resolution format.

ARABIAN FIGHT SEGA/1992

A beat 'em up for up to four players, this game was filled with many gorgeous details. It ended up competing with Taito's *Arabian Magic* (see page 192), also a four-player beat 'em up with an Arabian theme and released in the same year.

The typeface above takes inspiration from calligraphy, which you can see in the strokes at the top left and bottom right of many letters, and in strong diagonal movements as with P, 3 and c.

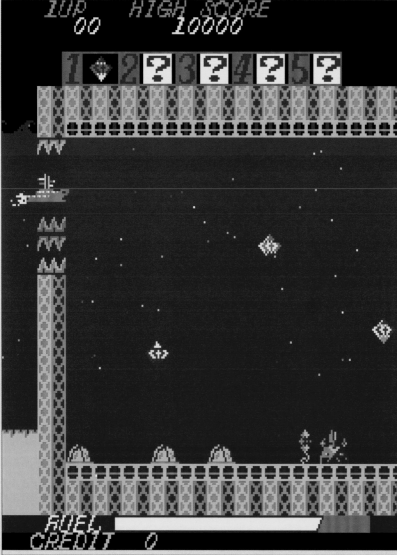

MARINER AMENIP/1981

An underwater horizontal shooter, infamous for its dreadful attract mode in which the player's submarine quickly crashes. The true value of the game is the fact that it has the first 8×8 italic face in arcade history. Unfortunately, the letterforms are quite rough, so each letter crashes into the next, and the stems vary in thickness. It is overly ambitious for a single-colour design.

07 CALLIGRAPHY & LETTERING

SKY FOX JALECO/NICHIBUTSU USA/1987

In *Sky Fox*, players pilot a space fighter jet and shoot showgirls, who sometimes appear on a giant serpent. Needless to say the game was criticized for its choice of enemy characters. This beautiful Roundhand script is too good to be the typeface for this game. Darker grey pixels are used cleverly as thin strokes, and the varying degree of the slant helps to make great use of every tile.

CAMELTRY TAITO/1989

This fun handwritten-style typeface appears on the game's tutorial screen. Between 1989 and 2000, the North American arcade market mandated the inclusion of an anti-drug slogan that said 'winners don't use drugs' in game attract modes. This FBI drug screen became a staple of 90s arcade games in the US. The font above and one other unique blocky sans comprise the two main typographic toolkits of the game.

SHADOW DANCER SEGA/1989

This sequel to *Shinobi* (see page 184) is similar to the original game, with the addition of a ninja dog. In contrast to the original font, which had a Japanese style, this version incorporates elements of Western calligraphy into its design. The typeface gives the impression of being written with a hard nib instead of a brush, the direction of the strokes is upwards and to the right just like Chancery Italic, and the characters have traditional proportions. The shading and colour choices here are more subtle than in the *Shinobi* face and create a 3D effect.

THE NINJA KIDS TAITO/1990

In *The Ninja Kids*, players control ninja dolls with swords, sickles and throwing stars, attacking Satanist dolls on the streets of America. This slanted face seems to be the work of a Taito developer with a passion for italics. Interestingly, the lowercase q is often the letter Japanese developers pay close attention to, perhaps this is related to how they were taught to write in school. Elsewhere in the game, there is also a very good 16×16 adaptation of Letraset's Quicksilver (1976).

07 CALLIGRAPHY & LETTERING

THE SIMPSONS KONAMI/1991

Konami could do no wrong in the 90s, especially when it came to franchise beat 'em ups. The typeface for this game captures the lettering from the credits of the TV show perfectly, making free use of slanting letters left and right. The exaggerated slant effect helps to narrow letters like I and J to occupy their tile, reducing any spacing problems.

WARRIOR BLADE: RASTAN SAGA EPISODE III TAITO/1991

Rastan Saga finally has an appropriate typeface in this game, after the strangely attractive, but thematically ill-fitting, geometric sans in *Nastar*, AKA *Rastan Saga II* (see page 250). The lively italic caps with rather vulgar strokes are a harmonious match for the tone of the game. There is a noticeable similarity between this typeface and those used in other Taito games released around the same time, especially *Pu·Li·Ru·La* (see page 189), in letters like D, Z and 9. It is likely that they were designed by the same person.

ASTERIX KONAMI/1992

Another great franchise-based beat 'em up from Konami. The font captures the characteristics of the comic-book lettering well, the most crucial being the dot above the I. This small detail may not seem very important to readers in America or Japan, where *Asterix* was never popular, but it is an iconic typographic feature of the series.

181

VENTURE
EXIDY/1981

SHINOBI
SEGA/1987

1P　　　　　0　　HIGH　60000

SHINOBI

INSERT COIN

SEGA 1987

SAVE

2:41

SHINOBI SEGA/1987

Ninjas in Japanese entertainment were cartoon characters, and all ninja games in the arcade before 1987 featured cutesy mascots and cutesy typography. The American ninja craze started in the 80s and reimagined ninjas as modern and mysterious heroes, an idea that Japan then reappropriated. This amazing bottom-heavy typeface reflects brush styles from American ninja films, using only one colour and the full 8-pixel height of each tile.

NATURALLY, THOSE IN POWER
REFUSED.
AND ALL THE TOWNS OPPOSING
THE KING WERE DESTROYED
BY THE KING'S MAGIC.

SOME PEOPLE ENGAGED THE KING
IN MAN-TO-MAN COMBAT TO SAVE
THEIR TOWNS.
BUT ALL CHALLENGERS PERISHED
IN A SEA OF BLOOD BEFORE THIS
SWORDSMAN KING, WHO CLAIMED
TO BE THE STRONGEST MAN ALIVE.

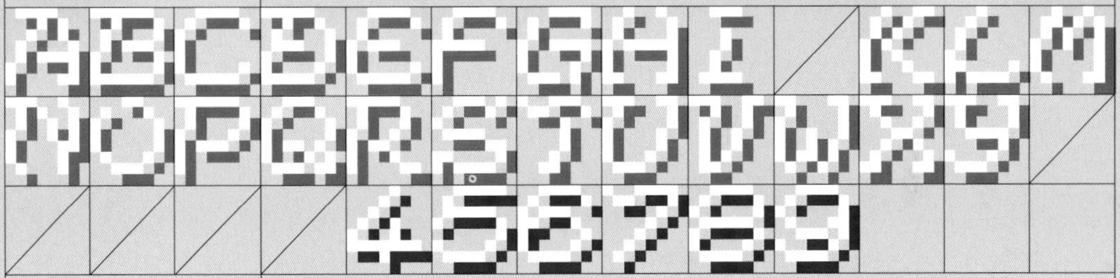

ABCDEFGHI KLM
NOPQRSTUVWXY
456789

BLANDIA ALLUMER/1992

The sequel to Taito's *Gladiator* (see page 243) was created at the beginning of the fighting-game craze. The main typeface was an outlined sans from the Depthcharge (see page 19) branch of typography. The face pictured above is displayed in the story and high-score screens, and only includes the necessary characters. It is unfortunate that it is incomplete, as it is a very good design. The punctuation has blue shadows, a cool effect rather than a necessary emphasis.

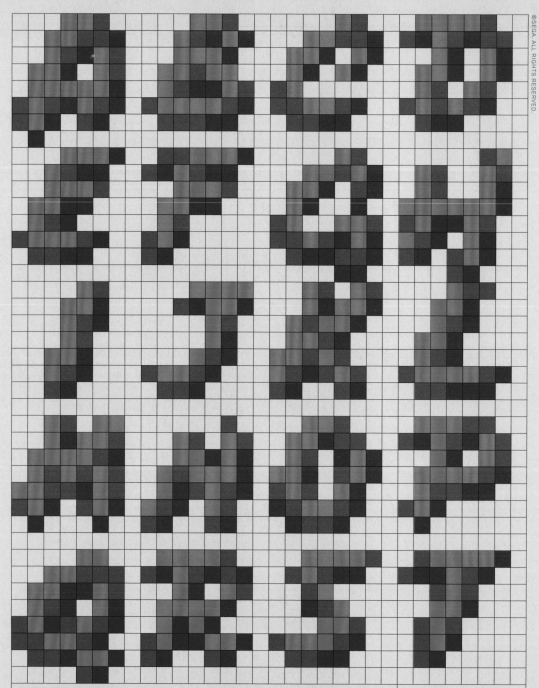

LASER GHOST SEGA/1990

A lightgun shooter with a comical setting in which players attack ghosts. The typeface has the feel of casual handwriting à la Roger Excoffon, who is known for the Mistral (1953) and Choc (1955) typefaces. It is an impressive piece of work, and the three colours are well used to give it a brushy texture.

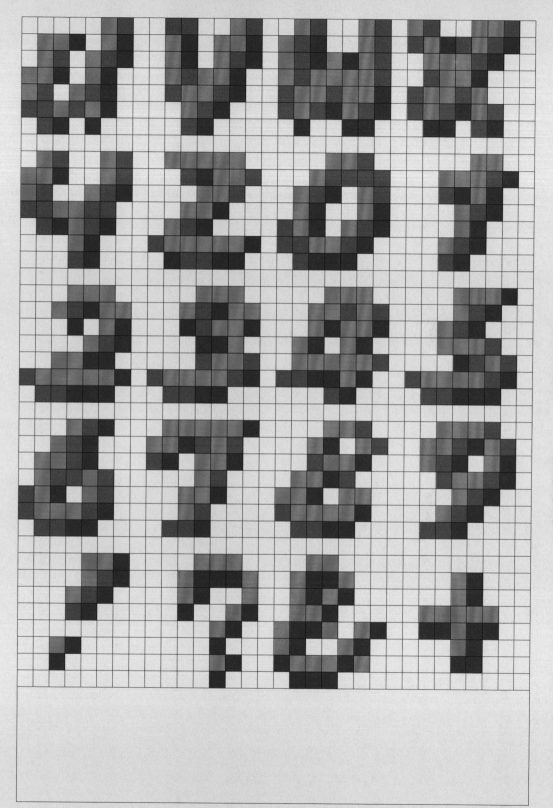

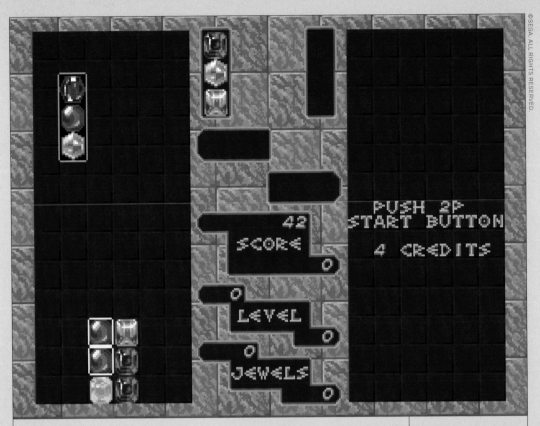

PUSH 2P
START BUTTON

4 CREDITS

42
SCORE
0

0
LEVEL
0

0
JEWELS
0

ABCDEFGHIJKLM
NOPQRSTUVWXYZ
0123456789

COLUMNS SEGA/1990

Sega's famous match-three game in which the theme of ancient Greece is communicated through close attention to detail in the lettering style. The letter O, for example, has a single pixel at its centre to mimic the letter Theta, which has a bar or dot inside the circle. Letters like E and P were often written or carved in stone with triangular proportions, a characteristic which is recreated exactly here.

PU·LI·RU·LA TAITO/1991

In a world where the flow of time is controlled by the Time Key, a bad guy shows up to steal it. Players are on a mission to save the world in this adorable beat 'em up with an abundance of bizarre enemies and stages, including giant elephant-spewing female legs that were later banned outside of Japan. This handwritten typeface is perfect for the picture-book style of the game.

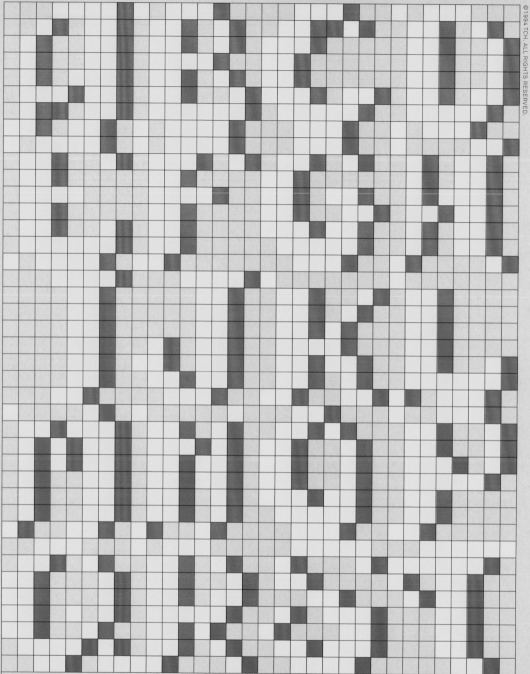

MONSTERS WORLD TCH/1994

A *Pang* (see page 112) clone made by Spanish developer TCH. The designer of this typeface has been heavily influenced by *Ghosts 'n Goblins*. The capital height is strictly aligned, which makes some letters, like K, L and N, look smaller than the others. However, this visual height discrepancy works in the font's favour.

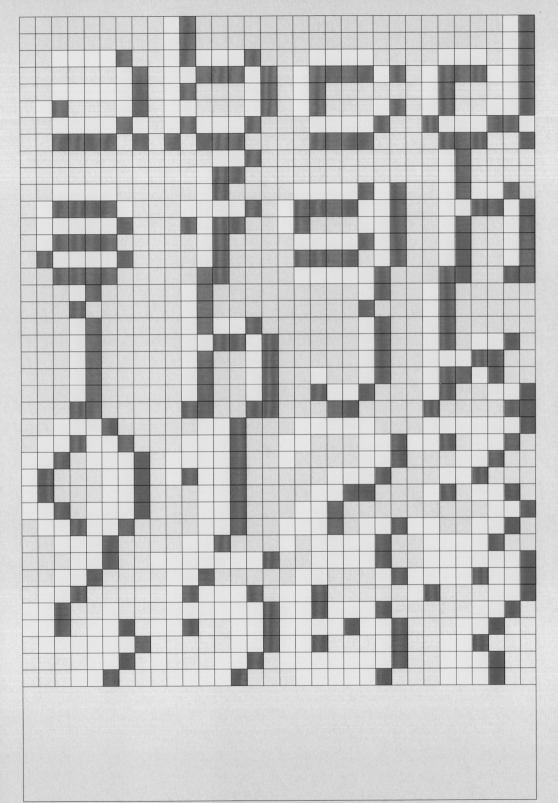

ARABIAN MAGIC TAITO JAPAN/1992

In the case of this Middle Eastern-style beat 'em up, the designers could have been tempted to copy elements of Arabic letterforms and convert them into a Latin alphabet. However, that kind of literal adaptation is often disastrous.

Instead, this typeface adopts Arabic visual patterns much more loosely, which makes for a more legible and effective font. The capitals here look more successful than the slanted lowercase.

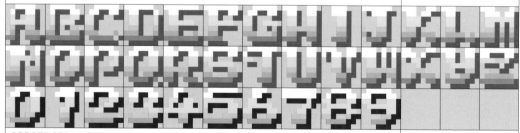

METAMORPHIC FORCE KONAMI/1993

A side-scrolling beat 'em up with up to four player characters who can collect power-ups and transform into beasts.

This beautiful Art Nouveau font appears to be based on an Arnold Böcklin typeface, but with a lot of smart adaptations.

SORCER STRIKER RAIZING/1993

Sorcer Striker was the first game from Raizing, a Japanese developer famous for quality shoot 'em ups. The steampunk art direction is unique and colourful, and the typeface design is a mixture

of medieval calligraphy and Art Nouveau. It is hard to say precisely what aesthetic the developers were trying to achieve, but this is forgiven due to the ambiguity of the 8×8 format.

07 CALLIGRAPHY & LETTERING

LIGHT BRINGER TAITO/1993

Who would have thought one could design an uncial font within the bounds of an 8×8-pixel grid? Taito did, and made a fair adaptation of Victor Hammer's American Uncial (1943) in their game *Light Bringer*. Unfortunately, apart from in the U and W, there is no trace of Hammer's typeface in the capitals. However, the lowercase is charming. Save for the descending letters being raised, it does a very good job of capturing the characteristics of Uncial.

QUAKE TOURNAMENT ARCADE LAZER-TRON/ID SOFTWARE/1998

Only a small run of twenty cabinet prototypes were made to house the arcade version of *Quake*. Its typeface has a sharp and slightly rusted metallic design with stroke contrast to match the biomechanical theme of the game.

The *Quake* logo is replicated in the Q, which is an unforgettable detail for any typographer who played the game. The small caps look natural and faithful to their larger counterparts.

GALS PANIC II KANEKO/1993

Publications in the 70s and 80s were revolutionized by dry transfer lettering, more commonly known as Letraset. This Lombardic capital set with a pink candy-like texture mirrors pornographic magazines of the time. It captures the historical model very well, save for the narrow N and R. There are no historical models for Arabic numerals, but those included here don't look too bad.

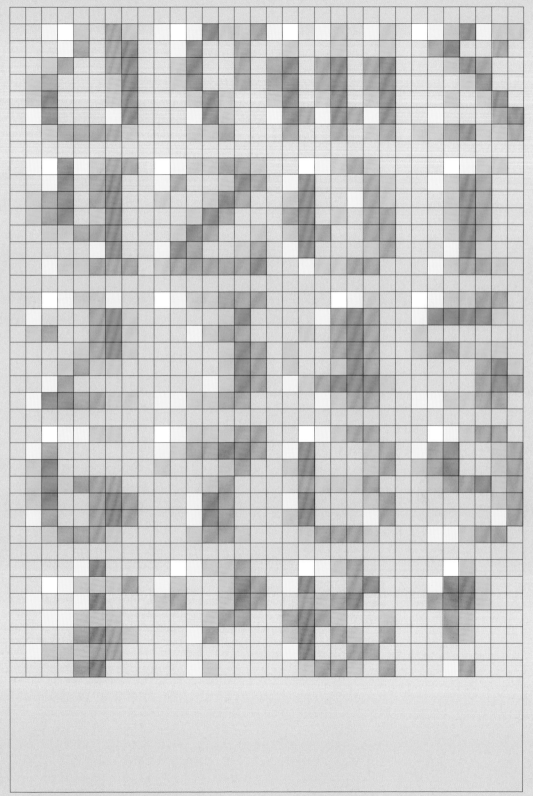

THE SIMPSONS
KONAMI/1991

LIGHT BRINGER
TAITO / 1993

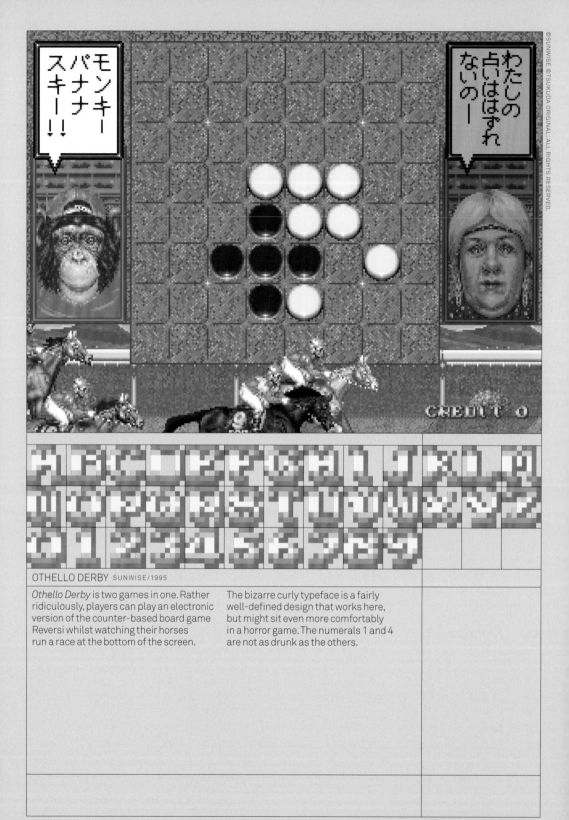

OTHELLO DERBY SUNWISE/1995

Othello Derby is two games in one. Rather ridiculously, players can play an electronic version of the counter-based board game Reversi whilst watching their horses run a race at the bottom of the screen.

The bizarre curly typeface is a fairly well-defined design that works here, but might sit even more comfortably in a horror game. The numerals 1 and 4 are not as drunk as the others.

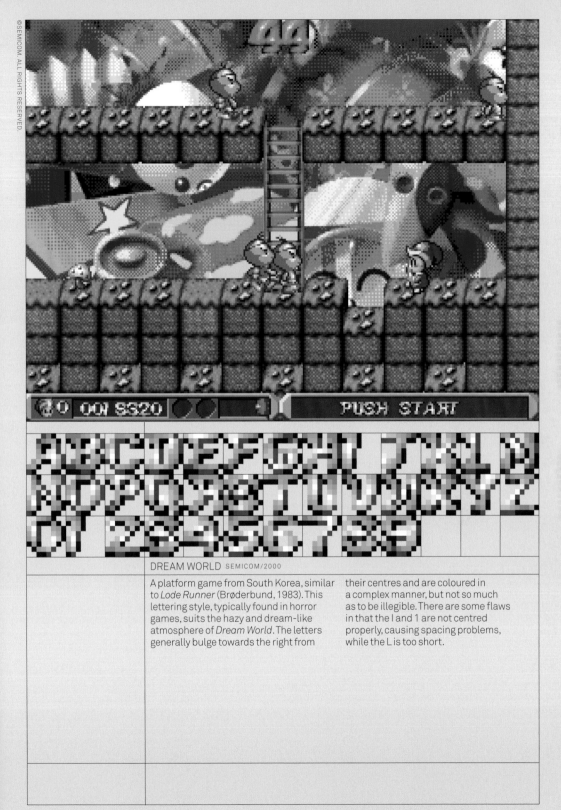

DREAM WORLD SEMICOM/2000

A platform game from South Korea, similar to *Lode Runner* (Brøderbund, 1983). This lettering style, typically found in horror games, suits the hazy and dream-like atmosphere of *Dream World*. The letters generally bulge towards the right from their centres and are coloured in a complex manner, but not so much as to be illegible. There are some flaws in that the l and 1 are not centred properly, causing spacing problems, while the L is too short.

08

HORIZONTAL STRESS

AGENT SUPER BOND SIGNATRON USA / 1985

A psychedelic maze shooter, advertised as being similar to *Elevator Action* (Taito, 1983) – but actually very different. Horizontally stressed type can be made by adding weight at the top and bottom, and this typeface is an anatomical example of this. It is a very strange font that seems to be using serifs with a thickness that is not always two pixels. The colour choices, though fitting for the game, are too vivid.

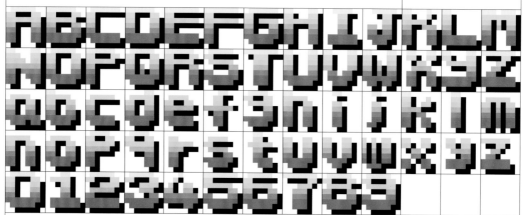

HEAVY METAL SEGA / 1985

Sega's obsession with outlining their fonts started in 1985 and lasted for a long time. Outlines take up two pixels around a letterform, reducing the working space to 6×6 pixels at most. This tank combat game has a solid, bottom-heavy sans with an explosive colour palette. However, the distinction of just one pixel between O and Q is not enough.

WONDER BOY ESCAPE / SEGA / 1986

Also known as *Adventure Island*, this side-scrolling action game features a caveman on a skateboard. The typeface is a bottom-heavy sans with a high waist. The ascending lowercase g, p and q are substandard features in an otherwise beautiful design. The I with different serif lengths, Q with its middle finger detail, and the five-square x are charming oddities.

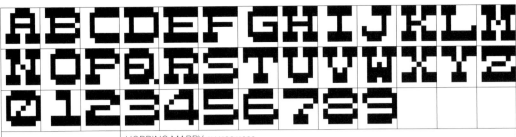

HOPPING MAPPY NAMCO/1986

A puzzle action game in which players control a mouse police officer chasing cats on a pogo stick. The typeface style chosen by Namco for the game is a horizontally stressed Roman, more commonly referred to as Western. Of all the Western typefaces in the catalogue, this one is especially true to the design principle it sets, with no deviation or multicoloured trickery.

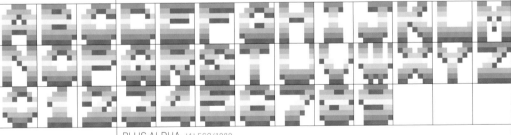

PASSING SHOT SEGA/1988

A doubles tennis game programmed into tabletop cabinets that allowed up to four people to play simultaneously. The typeface used is a new take on the developer's Heavy Metal font (see opposite) with extensive changes. The horizontal stress on the numerals has been emphasized, which works well.

PLUS ALPHA JALECO/1989

A vertical cute 'em up in which players control a rotund aircraft piloted by an anime girl. *Plus Alpha* was very popular due to its relatively easy gameplay, which attracted a more casual crowd of gamers. The typeface flashed constantly during play, but not on the name entry screen, from which this example has been replicated. The bottom-heavy design condenses the character details, and the asymmetry adds a subtle sense of movement.

CHEYENNE
EXIDY/1984

HOPPING MAPPY
NAMCO/1986

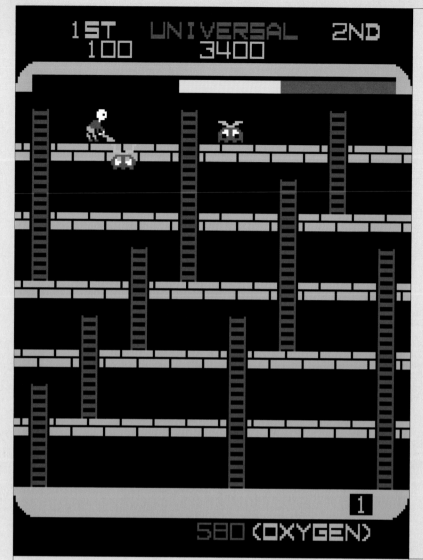

SPACE PANIC UNIVERSAL/1980

A single-screen platformer released even earlier than *Donkey Kong* and considered to be the original platform game. All horizontal strokes in the typeface are two pixels thick, a style choice made possible by occupying all eight pixels of height. The diagonals remain thin, which may be a result of using rigid logic to thicken the strokes. A different approach was taken in designing the numerals, but the use of curves is inconsistent.

SCORE1=00000   HIGH SCORE

SCORE2=00000   00000

=0   COIN=00

A B C / E / G H I / K L M
N O P / R S T U V / X Y
0 1 2 3 4 5 6 7 8 9

STRATOVOX SUN DENSHI/1980

The alternative title of this game in Japan was *Speak & Rescue* because it features voice synthesis, which was quite a novelty at the time. The debut of horizontally stressed typefaces was in 1980, and the *Stratovox* face was likely the first. Not all twenty-six letters appear in the game, but this is a cute little font that has one of the most unusual styles of the time, even though it could have been more consistent with the horizontal thickness.

207

LAST DANCE SALOON

100

O COINS   INSERT COIN   O CREDITS

CHEYENNE EXIDY/1984

A Western-themed lightgun shooter that appropriately uses a reverse-stress roman style. The serifs have more decoration than usual, as seen in the extra pixels extruding from C, G and J. The I has extra serifs just like the same character in Mouse Trap (see page 108), an earlier serif typeface by Exidy. O looks smaller than Q, which hasn't been drawn in the reverse-stress style, and the middle bar height is also inconsistent. However, the typeface does get credit for including details that are often overlooked.

2UP ‡‡   TOP KAZ   1UP ‡‡
           0   10000   0

PLEASE INSERT COINS

STAGE   8

DAMAGE ░░░░░░░░░░░░░░░░░░░░░░░░ DANGER

SDI – STRATEGIC DEFENSE INITIATIVE SEGA/1987

The typeface in *SDI* is more colourful and almost as effective as *Hopping Mappy's* in the stressed roman category (see page 203). The rather standard design of the numerals is regrettable, but they are suitably legible for a high-stakes game in which players must shoot down incoming missiles to protect the Earth.

LETHAL ENFORCERS II: GUN FIGHTERS KONAMI/1994

The idea of a Western game like this using a Western font might seem obvious, but there have been only two such examples in the arcade; the other is Exidy's *Cheyenne* (see page 208). The horizontal stress is not two flat pixels but one and a half using grey, except in the A. In the numerals, legibility has been prioritized over consistency. The lowercase has some debris, leftovers from other letters, but does not appear in the game and is probably just a placeholder.

PANIC BOMBER EIGHTING/HUDSON/1994

A *Columns* clone with a *Bomberman* (Hudson Soft, 1983) theme. It was developed for hectic gameplay, à la *Puyo Puyo* (Compile, 1991), and the visuals and music were similarly comical. The typeface is well designed too, with pleasingly contrasting thicknesses. The lowercase has no descenders and the g is pushed up, but it is not as noticeable since the ascender height is only one pixel.

BUBBLE SYMPHONY TAITO/1994

This extremely bold design shows little regard for legibility and doesn't hesitate to sacrifice counters, as in B. It would be great for large use, but not as the smallest typographic element on the screen. It was not used, which was a wise decision.

CHARLIE NINJA MITCHELL/1995

A run-and-gun game that was never released. This typeface is a bottom-heavy sans mostly, but sometimes it slips into serif (F, I, J) or stencil (A, H, h). The space between lowercase characters is nicely filled with varying vertical stems and effortlessly compact descenders.

DANCE DANCE REVOLUTION 3RD MIX KONAMI/1999

An excellent top-heavy design in homage to Excoffon's Antique Olive (1962–66). The typeface has a mild gradation, using thirteen colours in the base letterform, shadow and highlight pixels at the top left of each character. As a result, the letters feel gelatinous and fruity.

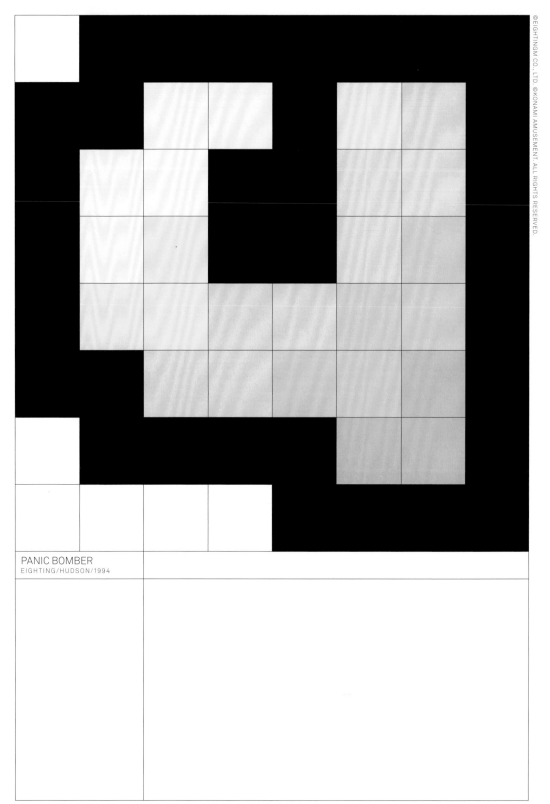

PANIC BOMBER
EIGHTING/HUDSON/1994

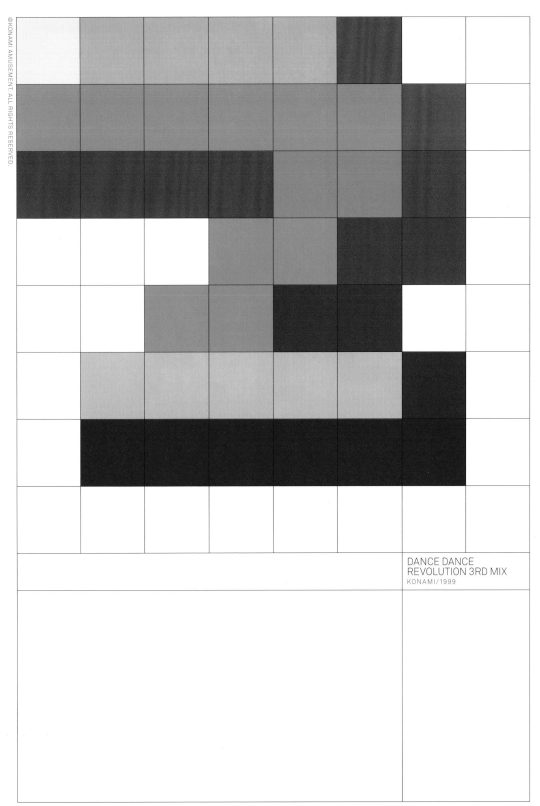

DANCE DANCE
REVOLUTION 3RD MIX
KONAMI/1999

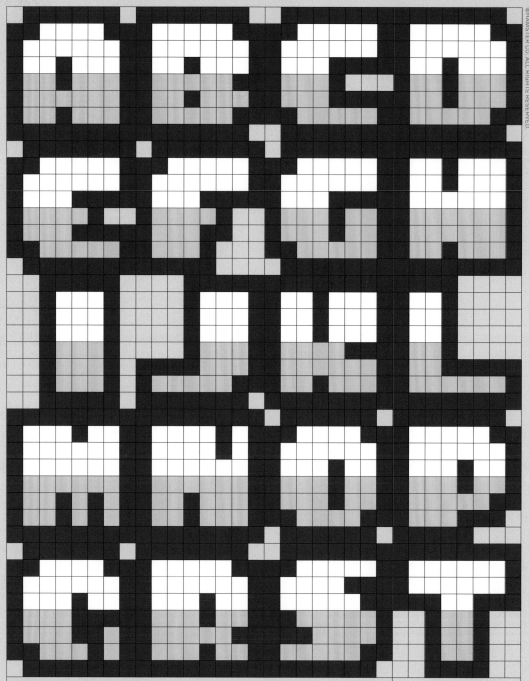

TAISEN MAHJONG FINAL ROMANCE 4 VIDEO SYSTEM CO./1998

A lovely outlined top-heavy sans that makes great use of the given space. The stencil lowercase is not in the same style as the caps and numerals. In the late 90s, online arcade play became commonplace, and players could finally enjoy a game of pornographic Mahjong against other real-life human opponents elsewhere in Japan. This is the fourth entry in the series, and there are many similar games.

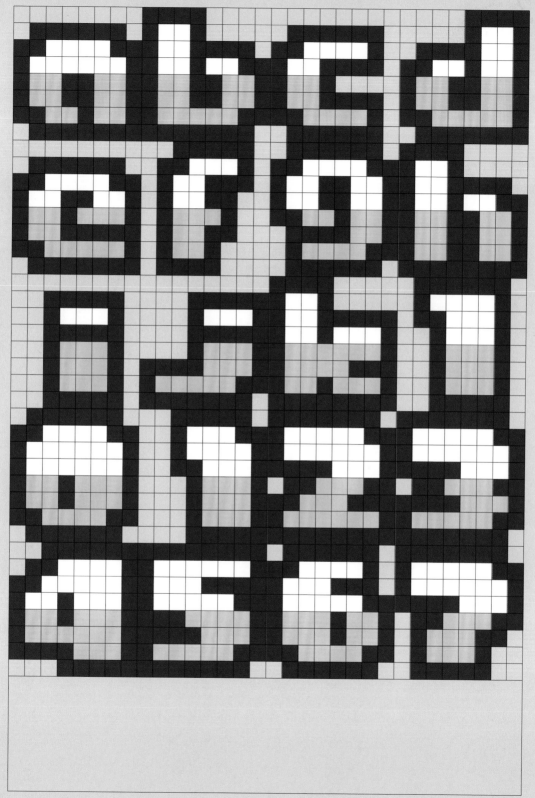

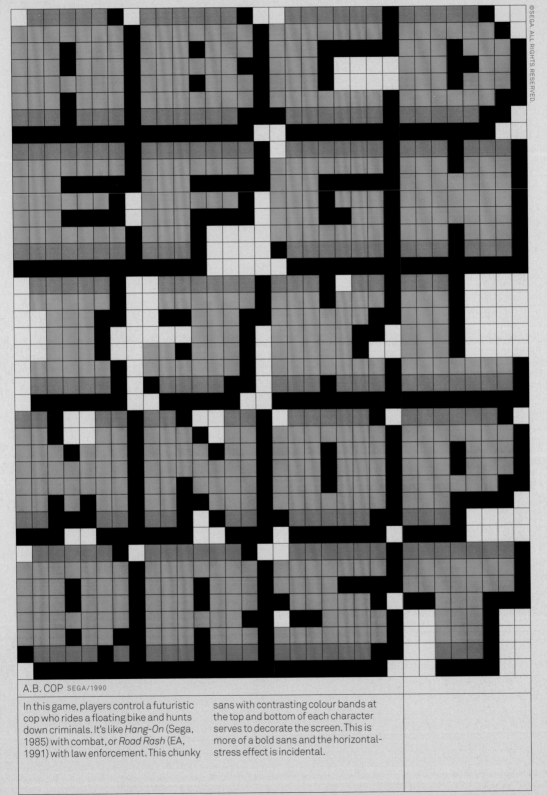

A.B. COP SEGA/1990

In this game, players control a futuristic cop who rides a floating bike and hunts down criminals. It's like *Hang-On* (Sega, 1985) with combat, or *Road Rash* (EA, 1991) with law enforcement. This chunky sans with contrasting colour bands at the top and bottom of each character serves to decorate the screen. This is more of a bold sans and the horizontal-stress effect is incidental.

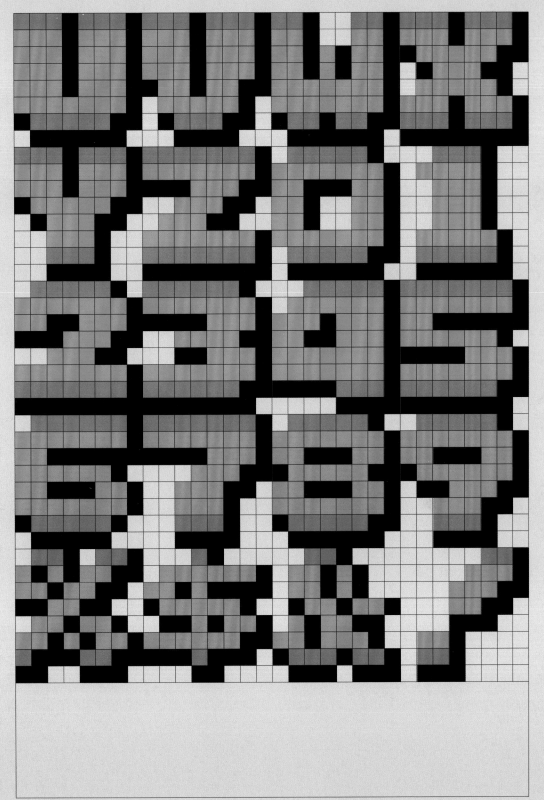

8×8 fonts form but a small sub-section of the typography found in arcade games and within this category this book contains obvious omissions, such as fonts from proportional and vector-based systems. Even the games that are covered here do not usually include just one 8×8 font in each, but have other supporting fonts and lettering styles. Here, we analyse two games – and every single piece of lettering in them.

BLOCKADE
Gremlin/1976

Early arcade games did not have leaderboards because every bit of memory space was precious. The graphic data of this early snake game is so minimal that the text portion doesn't really count as a font –there is a single character GAME OVER, the numerals 0 to 9 and that's it. The rest of the graphic data is for non-typographic use. Arrows in solid and outline fillings are used to differentiate between two players. The bricks are used as outer playfield limits, as well as your snake trail, while the halftone block blinks to indicate where the player has struck an obstacle and died.

1. The heads of players 1 and 2.
2. Numbers for counting rounds and victories.
3. Pre-composed GAME OVER word mark. It appears as stacked in the game.
4. Stage walls and the player's trail.
5. A cell that blinks at the player's crash site.

OUT RUN
Sega/1986

Out Run was one of the best-looking games of 1986. The player drives a Ferrari Testarossa through a variety of European vistas, with a beautiful soundtrack played through the cabinet's headrest speaker system. The game was created by Yu Suzuki, who had made *Space Harrier* the previous year. The 8×8 typeface was originally made for *Space Harrier* (see page 30), but the V is fixed here. It appears in grey, green and pink palettes. There is also a tiny version of the typeface that does not appear to be used in the game.

The 8×16 font is used on the leaderboard and for name entry and appears in yellow/black, lemon/blue, lemon/black and red/black palettes. Another set of 8×16 numeral fonts is used for the speedometer. Then there are the title logo and other miscellaneous graphic assets, such as INSERT COINS!, which is made up of custom lettering, with no other characters developed.

The origins of the game are evident from its unused graphic assets. Lurking in the code are ©SEGA 1985 and the same cool, blocky 16×16 font that was used in *Space Harrier* to announce new stages. The icon of Harrier (*Space Harrier*'s player character) is also included.

6. Title logo.
7. Leftover graphic assets from *Space Harrier*.
8. HUD elements for *Out Run*.
9. Speedometer font and music note for song selection.
10. Seemingly unused graphic assets.
11. Appears when a player reaches a checkpoint in time.
12. Coin prompts that appear during the attract mode.
13. Stage indicator at the bottom right.

6

7

8

9

10

11

12

13

14

0123456789.,€✦
ABCDEFGHIJKLM
NOPQRSTUVWXYZ
0123456789.,€✦
ABCDEFGHIJKLM
NOPQRSTUVWXYZ
0123456789.,€✦
ABCDEFGHIJKLM
NOPQRSTUVWXYZ
0123456789.,€✦
ABCDEFGHIJKLM
NOPQRSTUVWXYZ

15

©SEGA1985 ' " = ×
0123456789O◆◆◆✦
ABCDEFGHIJKLMNO
PQRSTUVWXYZ.

©SEGA1985 ' " = ×
0123456789O◆◆◆✦
ABCDEFGHIJKLMNO
PQRSTUVWXYZ.

©SEGA1985 ' " = ×
0123456789O◆◆◆✦
ABCDEFGHIJKLMNO
PQRSTUVWXYZ.

16

17

14. The 8×16-pixel typefaces for the song-selection screen, high-score screen, and remaining play time.

15. The 8×8-pixel typeface that was originally designed for *Space Harrier*. The pale parts are the unused leftovers.

16. 16×16-pixel typeface for *Space Harrier* to display stage names.

17. 4×4-pixel font, probably made for *Out Run* but unused in the game. It is also in all likelihood the smallest arcade-game font.

09

STENCIL

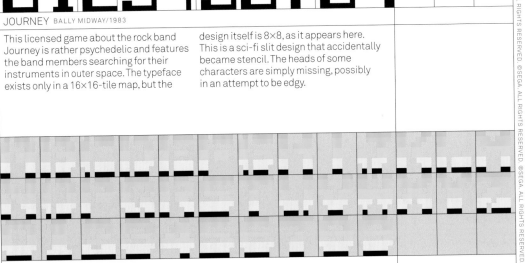

JOURNEY BALLY MIDWAY/1983

This licensed game about the rock band Journey is rather psychedelic and features the band members searching for their instruments in outer space. The typeface exists only in a 16×16-tile map, but the design itself is 8×8, as it appears here. This is a sci-fi slit design that accidentally became stencil. The heads of some characters are simply missing, possibly in an attempt to be edgy.

BULLET SEGA/1987

A top-down, twin-stick shooter. Unfortunately, its physical board is extremely sought after so is hard to come by today. The 8×8 typeface for *Bullet* is a stencil sans with a shadow cast on the bottom row only. It almost looks like a mistake, as if the black was meant to be white. It is a good stencil face, but could have been more throrough with the slits.

THUNDER BLADE SEGA/1987

A helicopter shoot 'em up with a creative pseudo-3D effect. The game did not see an accurate port until 2015's Nintendo 3DS version. This aptly themed typeface occupies eight full pixels of letter height, which seems to hinder the design more than help it, and the details lack finesse. The crossbars of E and F are both two pixels thick but look dissimilar, and P lacks the right baseline serif. The Z character needs two more pixels.

IMAGE FIGHT IREM/1988

Irem's vertical shoot 'em up *Image Fight* is famous for the very difficult penalty stage players enter if their kill rate isn't high enough. The typeface features common characteristics of sci-fi games, such as square design and 45° diagonals in the caps, while the lowercase was probably a placeholder. Stem thickness varies considerably from one to three pixels, which is too much, but helps to reduce the spacing problem, especially in I.

ACE ATTACKER SEGA/1988

A top-down volleyball game, only released in Japan. The game's primary typeface is a mildly interesting semi-serif that is no match for this secondary stencil font, which was only used as a novelty on the high-score screen. The face is not dissimilar to Josef Albers' 1926 font Futura Black with the addition of two pink shades. The W is too complex compared to other characters in the set, and it would have been better if the numerals were also in the stencilled style.

LINE OF FIRE SEGA/1989

Sega became more comfortable with creating stencil typefaces by the late 80s, and this is apparent in the 7-pixel-high sans pictured above. In comparison to *Combat Hawk* (Sega, 1987), another military-themed lightgun game, the *Line of Fire* face has a more mature design. The A looks as if it is leaning to the left, probably because of the crossbar, which looks more like a tilt than slit.

225

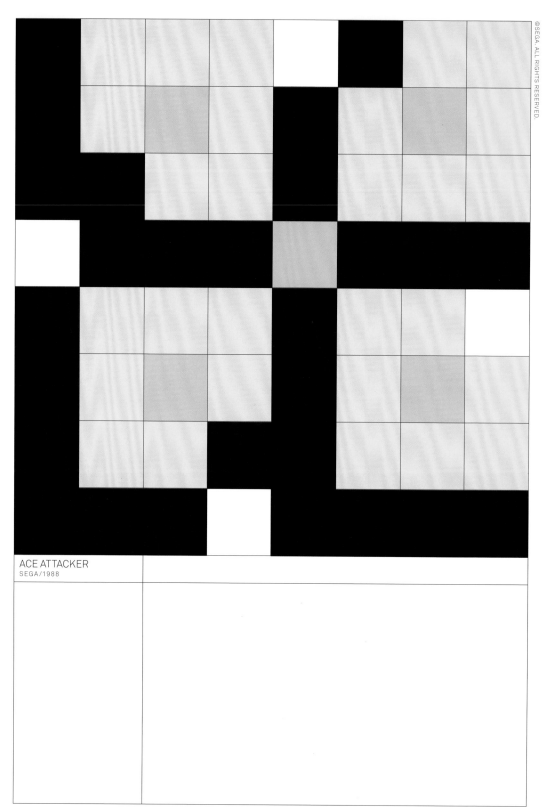

ACE ATTACKER
SEGA/1988

SUNSET RIDERS
KONAMI/1991

ACTION HOLLYWOOD TCH/1995

A top-down action and puzzle game that took inspiration from Hollywood action films. The typeface is reminiscent of the *Blade Runner* logo. The lowercase, despite not being in the same style as the uppercase, does not make the usual basic missteps that Japanese designs tend to. Overall, it's a neat design apart from the L character.

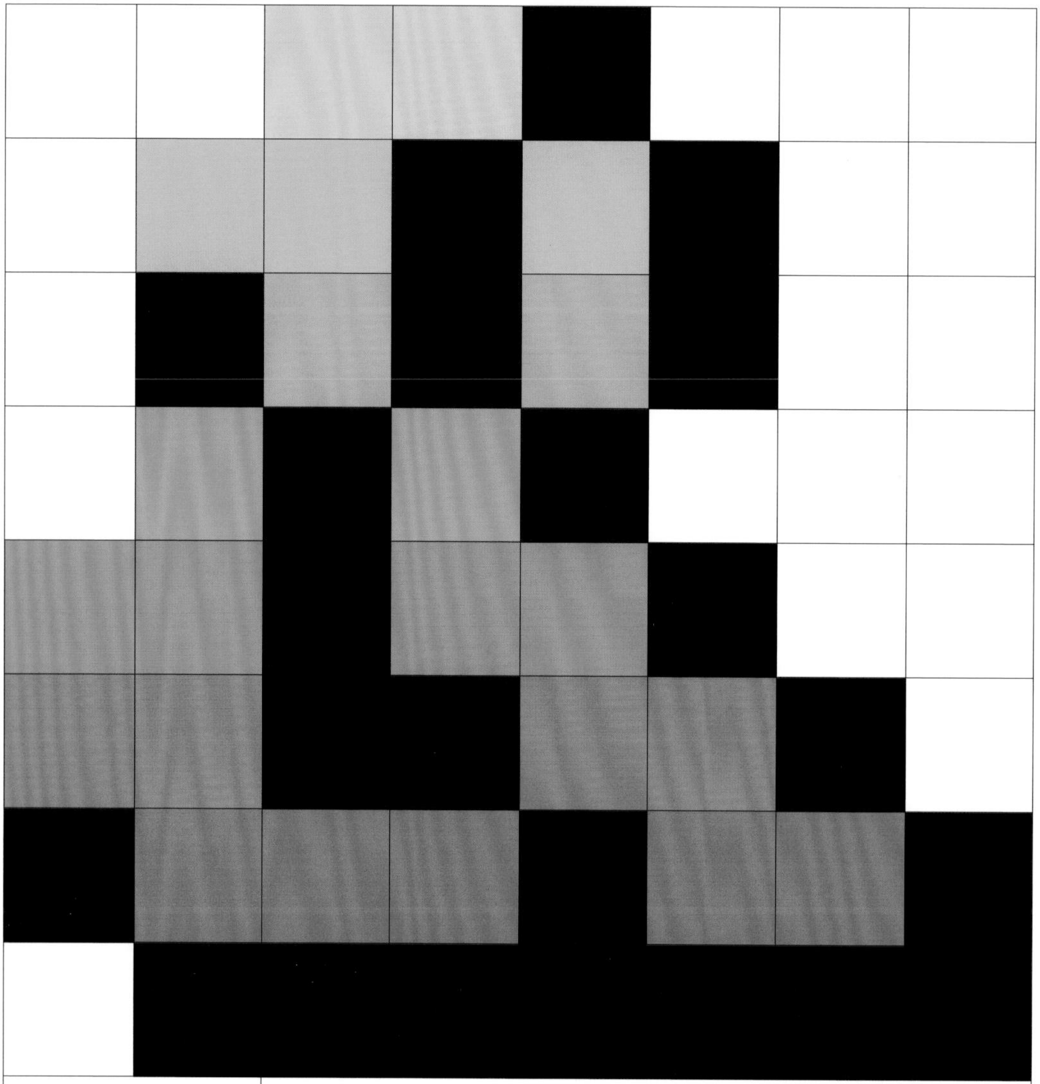

G.I. JOE
KONAMI/1992

09 STENCIL

KETSUI
CAVE/2002

```
BONUS TANKS GIVEN AT :
     10,000 POINTS

   SOUND DEMONSTRATION
   - - - - - - - - - - - - - - - - - - - -

LOW AMMO SOUND:
LESS THAN 5 SHOTS LEFT

LOADING AMMO SOUND:
PINGS = NUMBER OF SHOTS LOADED

FIRING BLANKS SOUND:
PRESSING FIRE BUTTON-NO SHOTS

BOTTOM LINE = SHOTS LEFT
       16 (AMMO : FULL LOAD
```

ABCDEFGHIJKLM
NOPQRSTUVWXYZ
0123456789

NATO DEFENSE PACIFIC NOVELTY/1982

In Nato Defense, players control a tank that travels through cities, trampling every stretch of maze-like road in sight. The stencil typeface has a rough design, but is appropriate for the game. If the slits were removed, it may look vaguely like the typeface used in Quiz Show (see pages 18 and 44–45), but the roundness, stroke thickness and spacing are inconsistent. It is not a particularly noteworthy typeface beyond the fact that it was the first stencil font used in an arcade game.

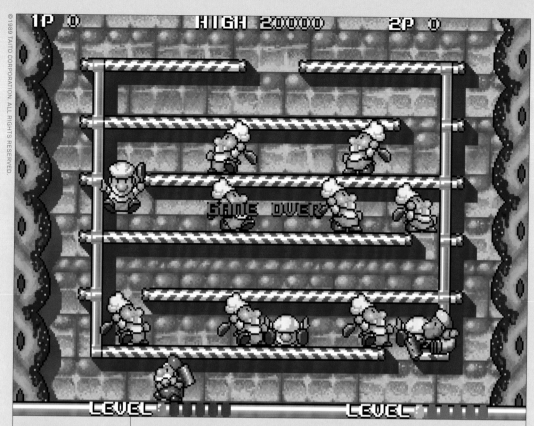

DON DOKO DON TAITO/1989

This typeface is roughly based on Quiz Show (see pages 18 and 44–45) but is stencilled, squared in proportion and more rounded in detail. It looks mechanical and futuristic, not what you would expect from a cute game such as this. It's an effective typeface, but would work better in a sci-fi setting. The font originally appeared in *The NewZealand Story* (Taito, 1988) with a lowercase and a complete outline, which was, of course, 9 pixels and drawn in a 16×16 grid.

BIG RUN JALECO/1989

This was the first racing game to feature the Dakar Rally. The player drives a Porsche 959, which was the vehicle that won the 1986 race. Strictly speaking, a rally game might not necessarily call for a stencil typeface. The decision behind the placement of the slits is stylistic, rather than practical.

AIR BUSTER KANEKO/NAMCO/1990

A horizontal shoot 'em up developed by Kaneko and published by Namco. The aesthetic and gameplay are not unique, but the game garnered favourable reviews at the time of its release. The typeface used is a realistic stencil insofar as the placement of the slits has ensured that there are no counters left isolated. It is not quite accurate, however, since a real stencil font, made using a physical stencil sheet, would have slits in characters like V in order to keep the inside counter stable.

GUN DEALER DOOYONG/1990

A tile-matching puzzle game, in which players can see naked women. The typeface above is seemingly unused in the game but is a nicely stencilled face nonetheless. Unfortunately the shadow is disconnected at each slit, which makes the letters less legible. Whether J should curl left or right is a genuine question if one grew up with a different writing style, and this is not the only instance of a flipped J – see *Munch Mobile* (Centuri, Inc., 1983).

THUNDER FOX TAITO JAPAN/1990

A side-scrolling beat 'em up featuring half-naked soldiers. This stencil typeface is only bold in C, I, T, U, X and Y, which is not too noticeable to the eye in the already busy set, and it also has an impressive

0 with a slash through the middle. The shadow applied to the top row is only sometimes present (compare B and E).

G.I. JOE KONAMI/1992

A franchise shooter, the gameplay is in fact a G.I. Joe-themed *Devastators* clone, also known as *Garuka* in Japan (Konami, 1988). The typeface used is also nearly identical to that of the original game,

apart from the different shadow shapes, the pixel on the bottom right in 0, and some added gradation. This is a good example of stencil slits being filled with a drop shadow, holding the letterforms together.

KETSUI CAVE/2002

A shoot 'em up with more of an emphasis on dodging the large number of bullets fired than shooting at enemies. *Ketsui* has two typefaces: they are both semi-

slanted vertically, and the main difference is the addition of stencil styling in the second face. This was one of the last typefaces made for the 8×8 format.

SUNSET RIDERS KONAMI/1991

Konami's *Sunset Riders* was an iconic cowboy-themed game in the early 90s and could be played by up to four people at once. The 8×8 typeface is a stencil serif with a back-leaning A, and the primary colour palette is golden. Not only did the designer make a serif, but they also added stencilling, shadow effects and diagonal gradation with shiny highlights. Perhaps the design is a little too ambitious and, as a result, the base letterforms are not as regular as one might want (see T).

CITY SWEEPER 001

CLAUDE
CODE NAME : LIGHTNING SLASHER
EX-KARATE MASTER

HE USED TO BE A KARATE MASTER AND HAD WON FIRST PRIZE IN THE U.S. CHAMPIONSHIP BEFORE. ONE DAY WHILE HE WAS TRYING TO PROTECT HIS GIRLFRIEND, HE GOT INTO A FIGHT AND ACCIDENTAL-LY KILLED A MAN WITH HIS BARE HANDS.

BIRTH DAY...
....2011.1.6
HEIGHT : 6'0"
WEIGHT : 172lbs
BLOOD...RH+A

ABCDEFGHIJKLM
NOPQRSTUVWXYZ
abcdefghijklm
nopqrstuvwxyz
0123456789

UNDERCOVER COPS IREM/1992

A city mayor decides to tackle the rising crime rate and begins to hire local vigilantes who are clearly not cops, despite the title of the game. While not an exact match, the typeface inherits elements from the *Image Fight* font (see page 225).

However, the angular characters, such as A, D and V, have been toned down and the designer has increased the thickness of vertical stems. As a result, this version feels a bit more grounded and less like it belongs in space.

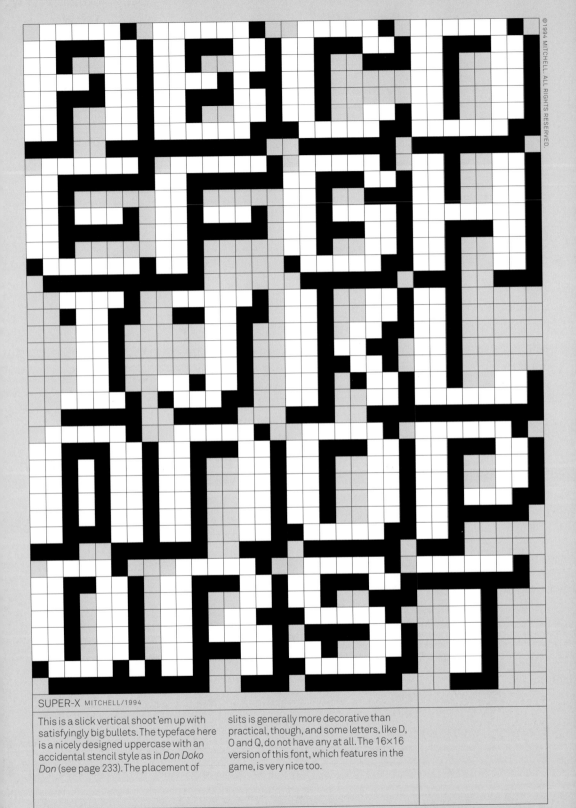

SUPER-X MITCHELL/1994

This is a slick vertical shoot 'em up with satisfyingly big bullets. The typeface here is a nicely designed uppercase with an accidental stencil style as in *Don Doko Don* (see page 233). The placement of slits is generally more decorative than practical, though, and some letters, like D, O and Q, do not have any at all. The 16×16 version of this font, which features in the game, is very nice too.

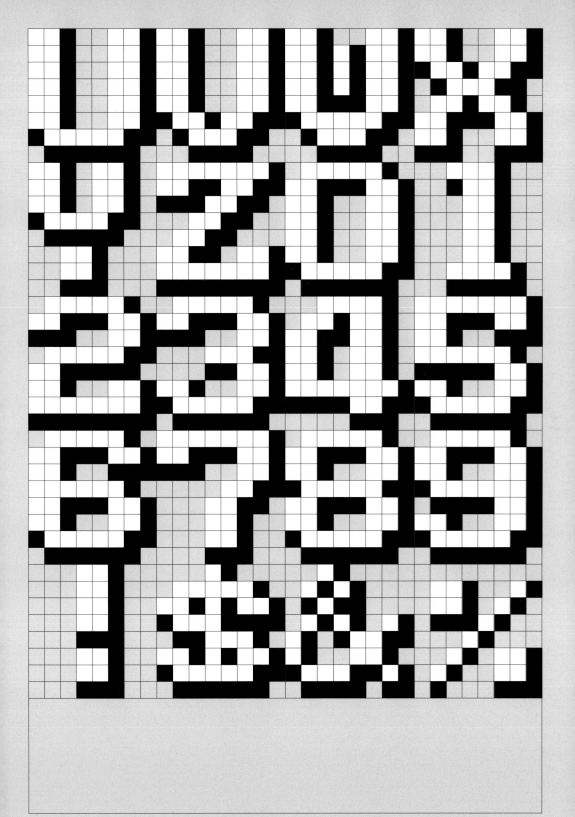

10

DECORATIVE

CALIPSO STERN/1982

Stern produced two very different typefaces in 1982. The first was featured in *Calipso*, an underwater treasure-hunting game in which players dive deep into the sea to shoot marine creatures. The typeface has indescribable stroke modulation and is consistently inconsistent. The characters fill each square space in a strange way, and the in-game appearance is not dissimilar to that of Morris Fuller Benton's 1910 typeface Hobo.

FUTURE SPY SEGA/1984

A rare isometric shoot 'em up. The typeface combines three different design ideas in one: stencil, edgy tops, and very diagonal numerals with strange stroke contrasts. Although these are nice ideas individually, they don't work as a whole and the typeface needs more focus. Strangely enough the pointed edges, especially in the M, foreshadow the font used in *Michael Jackson's Moonwalker* (see page 35), also by Sega. The six-year gap between them may be too long to infer a relationship, though.

DARWIN 4078 DATA EAST/1986

A standard vertical shooter with seemingly standard typography, until players reach the game over and name-entry screen that is, where this bizarre dualtone typeface is featured. If this font were to be made as a physical stencil, two stencil sheets would be needed. It is an interesting concept, but this particular typeface has lots of gaps in the strokes and has drawn in too many clashing ideas.

10 DECORATIVE

GLADIATOR TAITO AMERICA / 1986

In *Gladiator*, players control an armoured gladiator and attempt to beat their way through a horde of enemies. This typeface is used for the high score entry and ranking screen, while a solid white version is used for the rest of the game. The uneven highlights and shadows, along with the contrasting shades of dull teal and yellow, evoke a blunt and unpolished steel blade.

BLADES OF STEEL KONAMI / 1987

This ice hockey game uses a digital clock as the motif for its typeface, just like *Flak Attack* (see page 245), which was released the same year. Even though the typeface cleverly avoids ambiguity between B/8 and S/5, it is overall more literal in its approach and, therefore, not as successful as *Flak Attack*'s font. The 4 and 7 appear to be shorter because they follow the grid so rigidly.

OLYMPIC SOCCER '92 SEIBU / 1992

A gorgeous dual-screen football game that supports up to four players. Its roster of eight countries had nothing to do with the actual Barcelona Olympics of 1992 – only four European countries qualified, but there were six featured in the game. The 8-pixel font is what typographers call 'unicase', but the height should be aligned in proper unicase style, otherwise it's just a mix of letter cases, like this one.

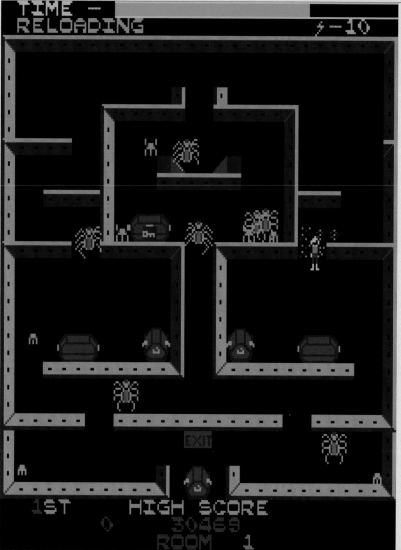

LOST TOMB STERN/1982

Lost Tomb and *Calipso* (see page 242) were both treasure-hunting games released in the same year. Their typefaces are very different, but also strangely similar, and it is clear that they were both designed by the same person. Unlike the *Calipso* typeface pictured above, *Lost Tomb*'s face at least had a unifying feature in its use of thick and diagonal horizontal strokes.

FLAK ATTACK KONAMI/1987

Making a digital clock typeface is not a terribly challenging task, assuming the designer can use a subdivided grid. But what if you only have eight pixels to work with? *Flak Attack* tackles this typographic challenge effortlessly. The designer of this typeface has made a subtle distinction at the corners where a more literal-minded designer would not (see B/8, S/5 and O/0).

245

FIREBEAST (PROTOTYPE) ATARI/1983

An unreleased prototype game with a very interesting typeface. Many of the characters pictured above have good calligraphic decoration in the thick stems but not consistently, so B, for example, is missing such detail, although it would be hard to make sense of four square holes. Despite its ambitions, it is unsurprisingly hard to read and not a successful typeface in many respects.

ALTERED BEAST

RANK	SCORE	RD.	NAME
1ST	50000	1	HKR
2ND	40000	1	UCH
3RD	30000	1	SAT
4TH	20000	1	HAG
5TH	10000	1	HAS
6TH	5000	1	TOS
7TH	4000	1	TAK

INSERT COIN

®SEGA 1988

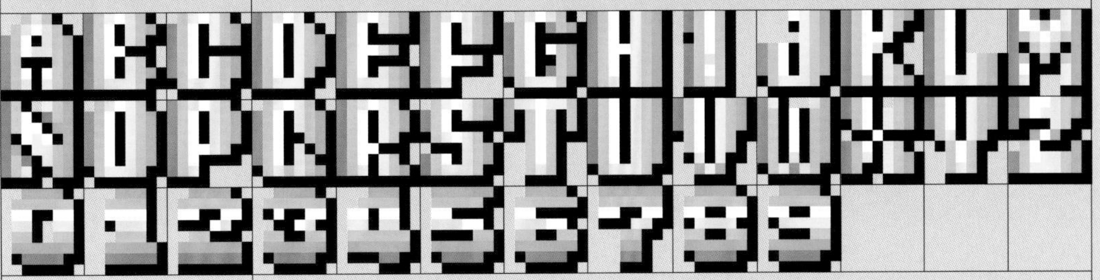

ABCDEFGHIJKLM
NOPQRRSTUVWXYZ
0123456789

ALTERED BEAST SEGA/1988

A side-scrolling beat 'em up with dragons and werewolves, and far better known than its typographic twin, *Ace Attacker* (see page 225). *Altered Beast* uses the same primary typeface, and this secondary face on the high-score screen, which shares the base letterforms with some alterations. The horizontal gradient on the letters creates a bumpy texture, whereas the numerals are gradated vertically.

RALLY BIKE DASH YAROU TOAPLAN/TAITO/1988

A top-down racing game. The typeface shown here was never used, which is a shame, as while the default font has its charm, it is nowhere near as good as this one. It is a chunky and blocky design with a deep 3D effect, and the counter-shapes inside are diagonal. The only difference between H and W is the height of the middle chunk. The K was absent in the data.

BIO-SHIP PALADIN UPL/1990

A horizontal shoot 'em up in which players can either move their ship, and have the targeting reticle follow, or lock it in place and shoot in any direction on the screen. The typeface for the game has a 3D embossing effect, which has an ambiguous boundary that makes it hard to isolate from the base letterforms. It's a unique typeface that can appear thinner depending on how you look at it.

GHOX TOAPLAN/1991

An *Arkanoid* clone in which players could move both forwards and backwards, an unusual feature for the genre. The typeface has an impressively detailed texture, and the vertical stems appear concave, like Hermann Zapf's 1955 Optima typeface, thanks to the darker pixels in the middle. The stem thickness could be more consistent.

10 DECORATIVE

GUARDIANS OF THE 'HOOD ATARI GAMES/1992

In this beat 'em up, the player is a vigilante in a neighbourhood with a gang problem. While the main typeface is the *Marble Madness* (see page 27) version of Quiz Show (see pages 18 and 44–45), there is another font, used for character introductions, that looks as if its letters have been punched in metal. It's a rare typeface, inseparable from its background.

RIOT NMK/1992

An incredibly hard game in which you fight an army that annihilates you by its sheer numbers. This typeface is secondary to the main typeface, which is also a thin roman, and appears on the high-score screen. Because of its notebook appearance, the background colour and underline of the typeface are part of the design.

REBUS MICROHARD/1995

A pub quiz machine, made by Italian developer Microhard. As with all of the company's arcade games, this contains erotic content. This typeface is used in Microhard's other games, but B is flipped. The letterforms that are bent in the middle do not cause spacing issues (see C, D, E and F), but the letters sometimes collide. The intention behind this colouring is not clear, but it does look cool.

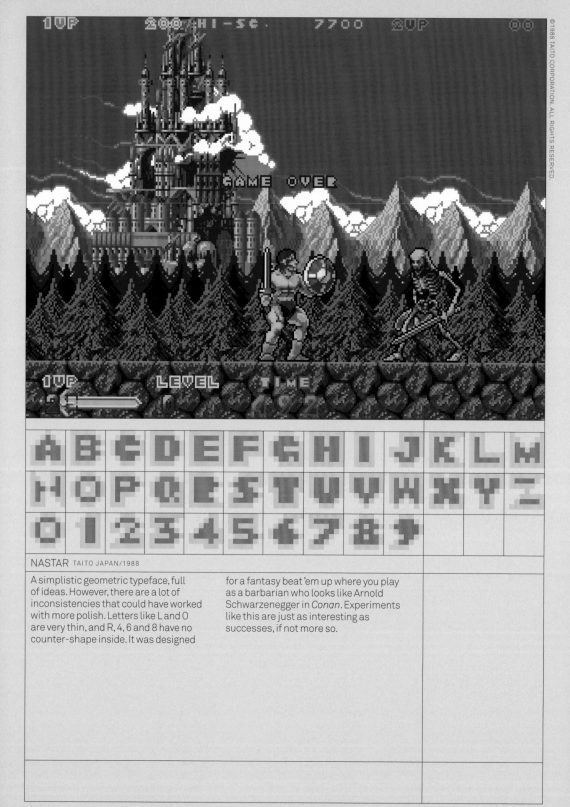

NASTAR TAITO JAPAN/1988

A simplistic geometric typeface, full of ideas. However, there are a lot of inconsistencies that could have worked with more polish. Letters like L and O are very thin, and R, 4, 6 and 8 have no counter-shape inside. It was designed for a fantasy beat 'em up where you play as a barbarian who looks like Arnold Schwarzenegger in *Conan*. Experiments like this are just as interesting as successes, if not more so.

10 DECORATIVE

GAME OVER

INSERT COIN

ABCDEFGHIJKLM
NOPQRSTUVWXYZ
0123456789&

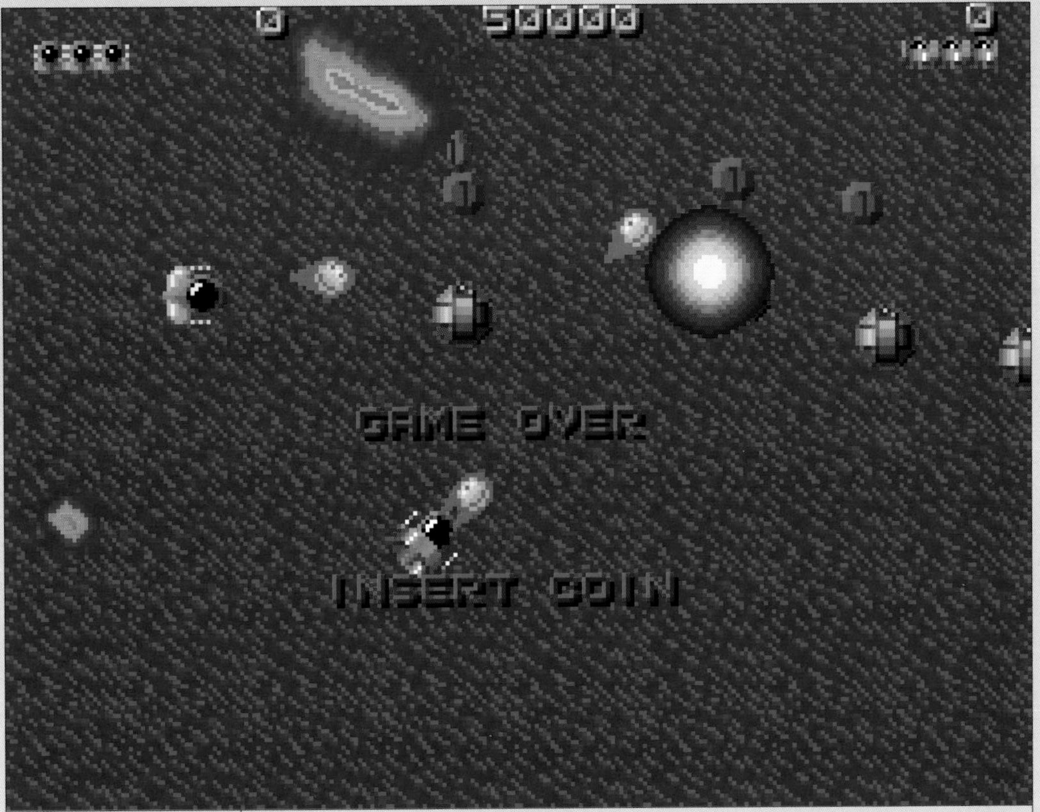

ARK AREA UPL/1988

UPL's catalogue is full of shoot 'em ups with varying degrees of typographic creativity. This is a technically impressive one that uses 3D to full advantage. Take a look at the S: there is no bottom counter, but the middle stroke is directly on top of the bottom. This would be impossible if the letterform was solid, but we can tell there are two strokes because of the embossing.

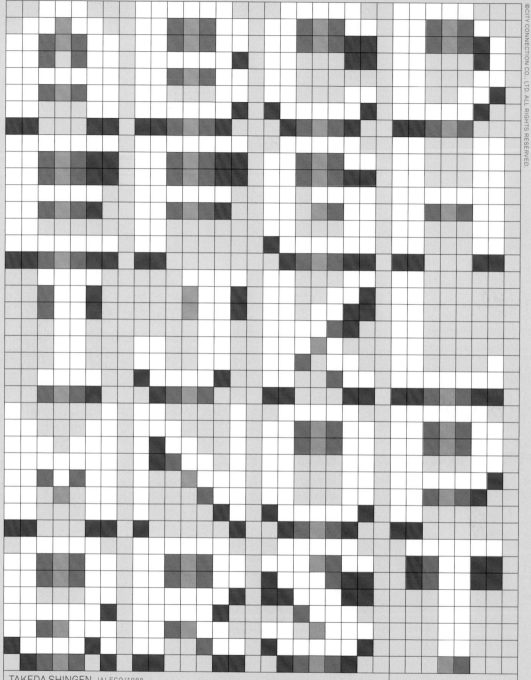

TAKEDA SHINGEN JALECO/1988

Takeda Shingen was one of the most popular lords in feudal Japan, famed for his skills in warfare. He also stars in this beat 'em up. The graphical standard is not high, but the typeface stands out.

Beneath some fairly standard letterforms there is a shiny metallic extrusion with differing heights, as if the letter is slanted forward, or the pillar of the letterform is sliced diagonally.

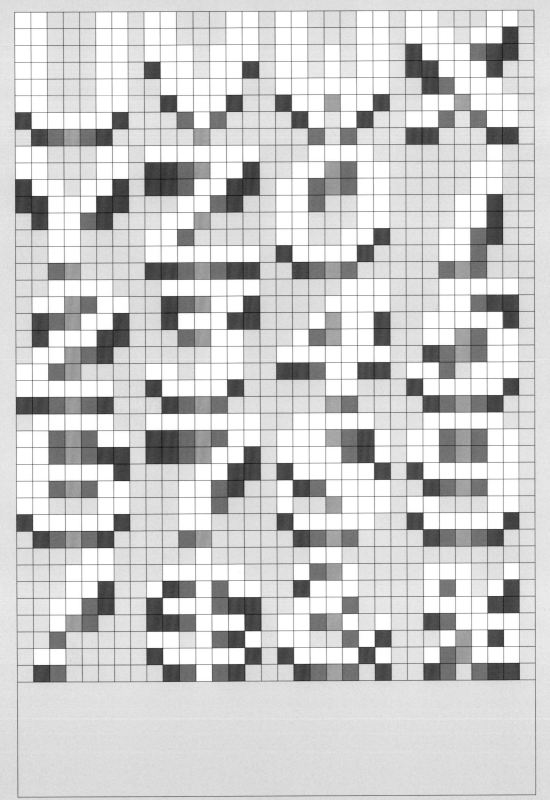

253

HYDRA ATARI GAMES/1990

Although Brignall's Revue has been around in games for a while, appearing in *After Burner* (see page 62) as a logo and in *Final Fight* as a 16×16 font, *Hydra* was the first to use it as a 8×8 font, and is probably the most faithful of the three. So much so that it even features the descending strokes of F and H that were present in the original. The lowercase is very well recreated, while the number 4 is a successful new take.

© BANPRESTO
© METRO

PUZZLI METRO/BANPRESTO/1995

A fishing-themed block puzzle. The typefaces used are all colourful and puffy, and look somehow appetizing. Within the two-colour outlines, mid-tone colours are used to great effect, allowing strokes to overlap each other, as in M and Q. The base letterform design is not strong or consistent, but the complex colouring totally makes up for it.

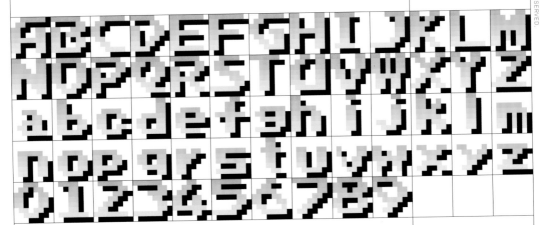

BUBBLE MEMORIES: THE STORY OF BUBBLE BOBBLE III TAITO/1995

This alien-looking typeface, vaguely similar to the Tifinagh (Berber) alphabet, seems unused in the game. It's not just a bunch of abstract signs, though – each glyph is related to its original Latin letterform. For example, E is rotated, M is copied to the top, and T is upside down. It is decipherable, but probably only when you know the design well enough already.

RAY STORM TAITO/1996

Called *Gunlock* in Europe, this is the sequel to *Ray Force* (see pages 142–43). While it does not live up to the earlier game, which had the best typeface, it is still nice looking, with stylish details like high waists, the crossbars of A, E, F and H sticking out, and diagonal gradation. The O and Q look very small.

WAKU WAKU 7 SUNSOFT/1996

A comical fighting game for the Neo-Geo system. The typeface is heavily inspired by Brignall's Revue, but squarer, and the lowercase does not have any resemblance. When it comes to the faithfulness to the original, Atari's *Hydra* (see page 254) takes the cake, but this is a better stylized adaptation of the classic typeface.

10 DECORATIVE

BATTLE BAKRAID EIGHTING/1999

The third and the last entry in the *Battle* vertical shoot 'em up series, whose previous entries used a MICR-inspired typeface. For this game, the developer designed a stylized sans, with a prominent diagonal cut and spike at the top left of the capitals.

FIRE HAWK ESD/2001

This vertical shooter, albeit in a horizontal aspect ratio, is its Korean developer's last game. The visuals were dated by 2001, and its sound has much to be desired. This bold typeface features diagonal corner cuts and dithered gradation, an effect that gives a rough texture to the letterforms and makes for a truly unique pixel typeface.

NIGHT RAID TAKUMI/2001

The closest typeface to explore the same genre as *Flak Attack*'s (see page 245) is from *Night Raid*, which is also a vertical shooting game. It is essentially a regular sans with an accented waist line and fragmented shadows, which is an easy but effective way to achieve the desired effect. The waist line has its own subtle gradation.

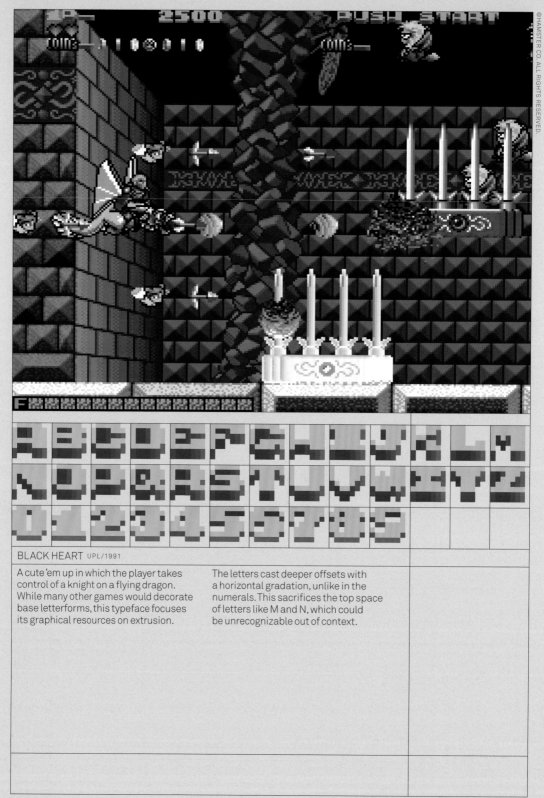

BLACK HEART UPL/1991

A cute 'em up in which the player takes control of a knight on a flying dragon. While many other games would decorate base letterforms, this typeface focuses its graphical resources on extrusion.

The letters cast deeper offsets with a horizontal gradation, unlike in the numerals. This sacrifices the top space of letters like M and N, which could be unrecognizable out of context.

PRIMAL RAGE ATARI GAMES/1994

A post-*Jurassic Park* fighting game in which you play as digitized stop-motion dinosaurs. The typeface is a glyphic sans serif much like Neuland and Lithos, perhaps influenced by *Jurassic Park*'s use of Neuland in its logo. Much like the backgrounds and characters in the game, it is photographic in style and suggests the use of CGI, at least in the early stages of the design.

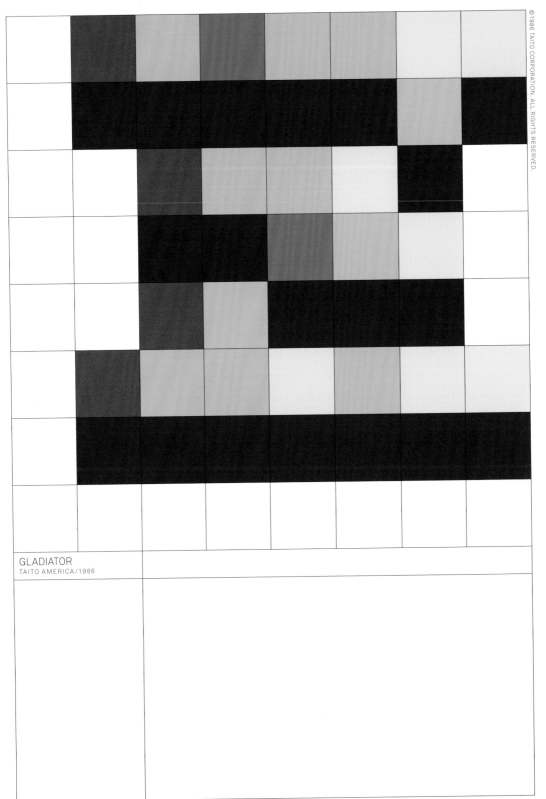

GLADIATOR
TAITO AMERICA/1986

10 DECORATIVE

NASTAR
TAITO JAPAN/1988

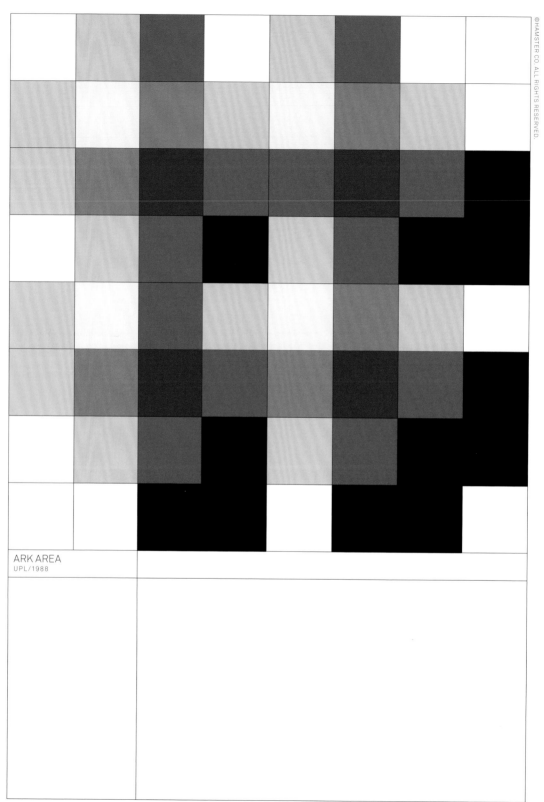

ARK AREA
UPL/1988

10 DECORATIVE

BLACK HEART
UPL/1991

THE END OF A FORMAT

The 8×8 monospaced format reached its pinnacle in the late 90s, when masterful pixelated works were commonplace. At the same time, fewer of these game typefaces were appearing, as bigger and more proportional fonts were favoured. Larger pixel formats were not new and you can even find examples as early as 1977. *Drag Race* and *Super Bug*, both by Atari, contained the first 16×16 fonts. Midway also used its own 8×12 font many times in the 70s. As graphic capabilities evolved, games became more complicated and demanded space for more individual on-screen elements. The standard text size initially reduced by the early 1980s and settled at 8×8 pixels for around two decades. However, as screen resolutions started to increase, 8-pixel fonts became physically smaller and their place was once again taken by larger formats. At the same time, the progress towards higher resolutions necessitated more flexible graphic assets. With the rise of photographic and 3D games, lovingly hand-pixelated artwork began to look out of place.

Higher pixel densities and advanced typesetting engines did away with the simplicity of the 8×8 monospaced format. Type design was no longer a job for game developers, and it became common to adopt existing designs instead of creating new faces from scratch. By the mid 2000s, when the Xbox 360 and PlayStation 3 were released, it was more efficient to use regular fonts in vector format than a set of high-resolution pixels.

This does not mean videogame typography has now become boring, however. Today's developers use their creativity in different ways. For example, in *Colin McRae: Dirt 2* (Codemasters, 2009) and *Tom Clancy's Splinter Cell: Conviction* (Ubisoft, 2010)

the developers have successfully managed to integrate text into the player environment. There are also more commercial interactions between the gaming and the type industries, through licensing as well as custom typefaces.

New typographic freedom brought with it greater risk of an inferior user experience. The Xbox 360 and PlayStation 3, for example, were the first consoles of the HD graphics generation, which made physical pixels even smaller. The text in the early games on these consoles was barely readable, because developers were slow to realize the limits of legibility. In their defence, developers were used to working to standard screen sizes in arcades and now had to adapt to variable home screen sizes. Digital displays do not contain information about physical size and so you cannot reliably reproduce anything at an intended physical size on different screens.*

Developers do know the target sizes when developing for certain devices, however. This is easy for a dedicated mobile device, but hybrid consoles like the Nintendo Switch require more thought, as its native screen size is 6.2 inches, but it is also built for TV use. You might expect developers to have optimized text sizes for mobile mode, but sadly this is not always the case.** Accessibility is a relatively new topic in the gaming industry, as the main consumer group has to date been generally young. Games with font size options are still few in number, but increasing.

Another cause of death for pixel typefaces was the 'Japanese-ness' of their spacing. Monospaced metrics are a compromise in Latin typography, unless there is a specific demand for it, such as programming or screenplay writing.*** On-screen typography was primarily monospaced in general, just as the first typewriters were, simply because this was easier and more efficient for engineers to deal with. Proportional spacing was always preferable and companies such as Atari and Midway quickly made layout systems to accommodate for this in their games. The 8×8 monospaced format had enjoyed unnatural longevity because of the dominance of Japanese developers, whose writing system was monospaced by default, and developers gave little consideration to the proportional nature of the Latin alphabet. This has now been recognized and monospaced fonts in Japanese games are becoming less common.

* In CSS, you can specify item sizes in so-called absolute units such as millimetres and, while it seems possible to display exactly that on any unknown device, it is not at all reliable in practice. In 2013, Type designer Nick Sherman tweeted an open challenge to render a $1 bill on a webpage at actual scale on any device, which remains unsolved. http://bit.ly/billchallenge
** *Doom* (id Software, 2016) and *Wolfenstein II: The New Colossus* (MachineGames, 2018) were both ported from home consoles to Nintendo Switch, but the company responsible for the port did not adjust the interface accordingly.
*** In screenplay writing, a general typography rule is to use 12pt Courier on Letter or A4 format. The idea is that a page should equal a minute of screen time if written in this format. This varies wildly in practice. For example, Tarantino's screenplays easily span several pages in a minute of screen time.

TOSHI OMAGARI

CONCLUSION

On-screen typography has now moved on to vector-based font formats and, apart from a few exceptional cases, there is no longer any need for games to use low-resolution pixel font formats. If they are used, this is usually an aesthetic choice or for the sake of digital archaeology.

Thanks to the worldwide adoption of emojis in the past decade, the big tech giants have come up with their own colour font formats: Apple's pixel-based sbix, Microsoft's COLR/CPAL and Firefox/Adobe's SVG. All have pros and cons and different reasons to justify their existence. The problem for pixel typefaces has been a lack of support, but this is rapidly improving and it should soon be possible to make coloured pixel fonts in any format and expect others to be able to use them.

For this book, the SVG format was used via a Python script for Glyphs.app, a program that converts a screenshot of a font into a real, SVG-flavoured Opentype font. HTML pages were built for Firefox and the book was typeset in InDesign CC 2018, which finally supports coloured fonts. The merits of using coloured bitmaps as fonts cannot be overstated. Without these applications, the production of this book would have been considerably harder, if not impossible.

You can embed animated SVGs in a font like the *Ray Force* (see pages 142–43) typeface, for example, and it looks exactly how it should on screen. Unfortunately, InDesign does not support animated SVGs, because nobody has figured out how to print videos yet!

We have seen the return of retro aesthetics in recent years, especially in the independent games scene, where pixelated fonts are used frequently. Most of these are made on modern architectures and are not designed in the same limited environment, only taking visual cues. The fonts used in newer games are also not literal adaptations of the old designs. If an old design is used, it is usually Quiz Show or some variant of it. *Shovel Knight* uses what appears to be Namco's *Pac-Man* variant with some changes. Developers seem to use black and white designs most often, despite the dazzling array of coloured fonts made at the peak of the arcade era.

We no longer use low-resolution display technology, and neither do we need native 8×8-pixel fonts, but in this severely limited canvas, such incredible expression was shown to be possible by artists who were largely unfamiliar with the intricacies of type design.

I believe experienced type designers can learn a lot from this brief but fertile movement of 'outsider typography'. The technology that hosted these creations might be long dead, but these typefaces remain as thrilling, eccentric and daring as the era in which they first enticed players to part with their spare change and press START.

INDEX OF GAMES

ACKNOWLEDGMENTS & CREDITS

For my parents, who inspired me to pursue a design career. And for my brothers and friends, who grew up together and built lots of memories around videogames.

Huge thanks to Owen Rubin, who is a former employee of Kee Games and shared his invaluable historical insight; NFG for his foresight to build one of the earliest collections online and for helping with mine; *IDEA* magazine and the former chief editor Kiyonori Muroga for publishing the great issue 352 about videogame graphics; Johney Choi for the technical help sourcing the images; Jamie Hamshere for bringing Quiz Show to my attention and providing me with historical references; and my designer friends who shared interests and memories with me, which kept up my motivation. Last but not least, my biggest thanks to Darren Wall from Read-Only Memory for this wonderful opportunity, as well as his incredible patience and guidance.

Kiyonori Muroga would like to give special thanks to Owen Rubin and Lyle Rains for information about the origins of the Atari font.

First published in the United Kingdom in 2019 by Thames & Hudson Ltd, 181A High Holborn, London WC1V 7QX

First published in the United States of America in 2019 by Thames & Hudson Inc., 500 Fifth Avenue, New York, New York 10110

Reprinted 2020

Arcade Game Typography: The Art of Pixel Type © 2019 Thames & Hudson Ltd, London
Foreword © 2019 Kiyonori Muroga
Text © 2019 Toshi Omagari
All typefaces © 2019 the copyright holders, please see the credits that appear alongside each typeface.

Designed by Leo Field

British Library Cataloguing-in-Publication Data
A catalogue record for this book is available from the British Library

Library of Congress Control Number 2019932292

ISBN 978-0-500-02174-3

Printed and bound in China by C & C Offset Printing Co. Ltd

Be the first to know about our new releases, exclusive content and author events by visiting
thamesandhudson.com
thamesandhudsonusa.com
thamesandhudson.com.au